Church Choices

Church Choices

Catholicism, Calvinism, and One Man's Search
for the True Church of Jesus Christ

JOSHUA SETH HOUSTON

WIPF & STOCK · Eugene, Oregon

CHURCH CHOICES
Catholicism, Calvinism, and One Man's Search for the True Church of Jesus Christ

Copyright © 2025 Joshua Seth Houston. All rights reserved. Except for brief quotations in critical publications or reviews, no part of this book may be reproduced in any manner without prior written permission from the publisher. Write: Permissions, Wipf and Stock Publishers, 199 W. 8th Ave., Suite 3, Eugene, OR 97401.

Wipf & Stock
An Imprint of Wipf and Stock Publishers
199 W. 8th Ave., Suite 3
Eugene, OR 97401

www.wipfandstock.com

PAPERBACK ISBN: 979-8-3852-5951-9
HARDCOVER ISBN: 979-8-3852-5952-6
EBOOK ISBN: 979-8-3852-5953-3

VERSION NUMBER 08/29/25

Scripture quotations are from the ESV® Bible (The Holy Bible, English Standard Version®), © 2001 by Crossway, a publishing ministry of Good News Publishers. ESV Text Edition: 2025. The ESV text may not be quoted in any publication made available to the public by a Creative Commons license. The ESV may not be translated in whole or in part into any other language. Used by permission. All rights reserved.

The Scriptures marked "NET" are from the NET Bible® https://netbible.com copyright ©1996, 2019 used with permission from Biblical Studies Press, L.L.C. All rights reserved.

To my father,

John Houston,

who left what he thought he knew
to be part of the one true church of Jesus Christ

Contents

1 Introduction | 1

Section One: Agreement and Disagreement with Catholicism

2 The Oneness of the Church | 9
3 The Universality of the Church | 20
4 What Did the Earliest Church Look Like? | 28
5 Salvation in Christ and. . . ? | 34
6 The Priesthood and Papal Authority | 40
7 Marian Dogmas | 46
8 The Rosary and Why I Own One | 52
9 The Canonization of Saints | 64
10 Purgatory | 71
11 Relics | 77
12 The Eucharist | 82
13 Where I Stand With Catholicism | 90

Section Two: Agreement and Disagreement with the Protestant Reformation and Calvinism

14 The Good and the Bad of the Protestant Reformation | 97
15 Luther and Grace | 104
16 The Doctrines of Election and Predestination | 108
17 Once Saved, Always Saved? | 116
18 Calvin and the Purpose of Prayer | 120

Contents

19 Calvinism and Baptism | 125
20 Where I Stand with Calvinism | 130

21 Conclusion | 134

Bibliography | 141

1

Introduction

THE PRESENT STUDY COMES on the cusp of two primary catalysts. First, artificial intelligence (AI) and large language models such as ChatGPT and Grok have become immensely popular. As a result, many preachers, theologians, biblical scholars, and secular inquirers have flocked to these sources to prove or disprove their doctrines. For example, a professor of New Testament at Faulkner University asked ChatGPT, "According to the New Testament—without creeds or denominational teaching—what must one do to be saved from sins?" The response was (1) faith in Jesus, (2) repentance, (3) confession of faith, (4) baptism, and (5) ongoing faithfulness. However, there is a problem. The way the question was phrased presupposed the response. I wonder what would have been said if the question read "According to the New Testament, what must one do to be saved from the wrath of God directed to sinners?" This is not a drastic change to the original question, but the omission of "without creeds or denominational teaching" would likely open the model to *sola fide* doctrines of Calvinism or the sacramental keeping of Catholicism. As AI tools become more common and as more people use these tools for their theological framework, more false teaching—or at the least surface-level teaching—will be done. AI models respond based on the formation of the question. What if we asked, "What must one do to go to heaven according to the teachings of the first five hundred years of Christian history?" I imagine there would be a greater emphasis on ecclesial duties given in the answer. I do not know. I

Introduction

did not ask. Maybe you could? The point is simple. Ask an AI question, get an AI answer. While AI may have its place, we do not want an AI answer. We want a biblical answer.

The second catalyst for this study is closer to home. I cannot remember the last time I listened to the radio. I imagine most of you might say the same thing. Like most of you, I typically listen to podcasts, audiobooks, and the occasional YouTube video (though I refrain from watching the video when driving). I was first introduced to Catholic-centric podcasts by listening to an episode of *Pints with Aquinas* due to its deep and provocative discussions of philosophical and theological issues. Subsequently, my wife began listening to *The Lila Rose Show* primarily due to its discussion of gender issues and its fight in the pro-life movement. The topics and method of discussion were unlike anything being produced by my own faith tradition. The quality of recording, the level of the guests, and the interaction of the host made these podcasts very enjoyable. However, many of the episodes would discuss Catholic doctrines such as the rosary, Marian admiration, the priesthood, the pope, and the Eucharist. As a biblical scholar, I wanted to engage with these teachings not necessarily to prove them wrong but to see if I truly knew *what*, and more importantly, *why* I believed what I believed.

The result of this process is the belief that I am catholic, but not Catholic. If you are reading this, you will notice the difference in how the word "catholic" is presented. The first instance uses a lowercase "c" while the second instance uses a capital "C." The lowercase-"c" "catholic" refers to the original use of the word before it was denominationalized. The word "catholic" comes from the Greek adjective *katholikos*, which means "universal," "general," or "according to the whole." In its earliest usage, *katholikos* was a philosophical term meaning "pertaining to the whole" or "comprehensive." The term was used in various Greek contexts to describe things that were universal in contrast to what was partial or specific. Aristotle uses *katholikos* in discussing universal principles that are always true no matter the context.[1] In describing methods of historical analysis, Polybius's *Histories* (second century BC) argued that a catholic view (*katholikos theōria*) of history was necessary for understanding how events are interconnected by looking at the whole rather than at isolated, unconnected events.[2] In ancient medical practices, Galen, a second-century physician, used the term *katholikos* to describe remedies that are used for whole-body,

---

1. Aristotle, *Metaphysics* 1004b25–35.
2. Polybius, *Histories* 1.4.1–2

general-purpose healing and thus not limited to one disease or body part.[3] Finally, the term *katholikos* was used by Christians as early as Ignatius of Antioch (ca. AD 110) to describe the universality of the church—i.e., the global body of believers united in Christ. He writes, "Just as wherever Jesus Christ is, there is the catholic church" (Ignatius, *Letter to the Smyrnaeans* 8.2). In that sense, "catholic" meant "orthodox," "united," "not sectarian."

There is no debate that the Greek adjective *katholikos* was used by early Christians to describe the whole, united church as opposed to heretical or schismatic groups. However, over time, the term became employed as a moniker for the institutionalized church out of Rome. By the third and fourth centuries, the term "catholic" was employed by orthodox Christians to distinguish them from heretical groups such as Arians, modalists, and Donatists. Cyril of Jerusalem (ca. AD 350) stated in his *Catechetical Lectures*, "It is called catholic because it is throughout the whole world . . . and because it teaches completely and unfailingly all the doctrines" (*Catechetical Lecture* 18.23). Even here, the use is not dependent on a so-called established sect out of Rome but on the universality of doctrinal orthodoxy.

The Nicene Creed is one of the most foundational statements of Christian belief. It was first formulated at the First Council of Nicaea in AD 325 and later expanded at the First Council of Constantinople in AD 381. It was crafted to articulate orthodox Christian doctrine in response to theological controversies, particularly the Arian denial of Christ's eternality and oneness with God. As J. N. D. Kelly notes, the Nicene Creed "became the standard of orthodoxy" in both Eastern and Western Christianity.[4] Affirming belief in "one God, the Father Almighty," and in "one Lord Jesus Christ . . . true God from true God," the creed sought to establish theological unity across the growing Christian world. It also affirmed belief in the Holy Spirit, the church, baptism, and the resurrection. The phrase "one, holy, catholic, and apostolic church" in the final paragraph of the amendment made at Constantinople clearly refers to the church's universality. The creed confesses that there is one true church. That is all it does. It does not inherently state that the one true church is the Roman Catholic Church.

The term "catholic" began to take on a sectarian identity with the Great Schism of 1054. The schism was between the Western church (Latin-speaking, Rome-centered), and the Eastern church (Greek-speaking, Constantinople-centered). Each claimed to be the true "catholic" church.

---

3. Galen, *De naturalibus facultatibus* 1.12 (Kühn 2.49).
4. Kelly, *Early Christian Creeds*, 297.

Introduction

After the schism, the title "Roman Catholic" increasingly came to refer to the Western church under the authority of the pope.

The Protestant Reformation of the sixteenth century rejected the Roman church's claim to universality but retained the term "catholic" in its original sense. For example, the Lutheran Augsburg Confession of 1530 affirms belief in the "one holy catholic and apostolic church," borrowing its language from the Nicene Creed. Protestants viewed themselves as part of the true universal church while separating themselves from Roman Catholicism. Today, the phrase "Catholic Church" (capitalized) typically refers to the Roman Catholic Church. Other groups that use the term "Catholic" in their titles include the Eastern Orthodox Church, the Old Catholic Church (which split from Rome in the nineteenth century), and the Anglican Church who often describe themselves as "Reformed Catholic."

Though I will not spend as much time on this topic as the previous one, it is necessary to discuss a similar issue with the term "tradition." Can *sola scriptura* (Scripture alone) really be true? To some extent, yes. The text of Scripture is the only extant inherent and divinely inspired message that we have from God (a detail our Catholic friends would dispute). This presupposition will be explored in later sections. Still, one must wrestle with the question of why Christians of all religious presuppositions practice their walk with God using tools and theological arguments not expressed in Scripture. For example, many Christians meet in church buildings—a phenomenon not found in the pages of the New Testament. Additionally, Christians sing hymns from a songbook often led by a song leader or worship director. No youth groups, senior saints' ministries, or livestreaming is found in the New Testament. So, if "Scripture alone" is true in its fundamental sense, these things cannot be part of the local worship practice.

For capital-"C" "Catholics," capital-"T" "Tradition" is equally authoritative as Scripture. Capital-"T" "Tradition" refers to the interpretation and passing down of Scripture throughout the history of the church. The Catechism of the Catholic Church (hereafter, CCC) states that the magisterium (i.e., the pope and bishops in communion) is the servant of the Word of God. They teach only what has been handed on through Scripture and Tradition and have the authority to interpret the Word of God but not to invent doctrine (CCC 85–87). If the church teaches a specific doctrine, the doctrinal teaching is authoritative regardless of hermeneutic discrepancy (e.g., the physical presence of Christ in the Eucharist).

Introduction

From a Protestant perspective—especially within the Reformed tradition—"Tradition" is not on par with divine authority. Instead, most Protestants uphold the principle of *sola scriptura*, meaning that Scripture alone is the final and infallible authority in all matters of faith and practice. While church traditions, creeds, and the writings of early church fathers may be respected and even helpful for understanding Scripture, they are always subject to Scripture and must be evaluated in light of it. Protestants generally affirm that only Scripture is divinely inspired and sufficient for teaching, rebuking, correcting, and training in righteousness (cf. 2 Tim 3:16–17), whereas capital-"T" "Tradition" is a fallible human addition to the authority already evident in Scripture.

This brings us to the title of this book. Scripture is clear that there is one God, one Lord, one church, one faith, and one body of Christ.

> There is one body and one Spirit—just as you were called to the one hope that belongs to your call—one Lord, one faith, one baptism, one God and Father of all, who is over all and through all and in all (Eph 4:4–6).

> For just as the body is one and has many members, and all the members of the body, though many, are one body, so it is with Christ. For in one Spirit we were all baptized into one body—Jews or Greeks, slaves or free—and all were made to drink of one Spirit (1 Cor 12:12–13).

> And above all these put on love, which binds everything together in perfect harmony. And let the peace of Christ rule in your hearts, to which indeed you were called in one body. And be thankful (Col 3:14–15).

What then is this "one church?" Who is in it? If we are in it, how do we know? In the chapters that follow, these questions are evaluated from a variety of angles. The book seeks to answer these questions in two primary sections. As I began writing this book, I quickly realized that only interacting with Catholic teachings would not be enough. Though I am technically part of the "Protestant" movement as far as the term "Protestant" refers to not being Roman Catholic, I admit that "Protestant" does not define what I am, either. Contrary to the views of this book's critics, I am not anti-Catholic. I am pro-true body of Christ. Thus, I find it necessary for the second section to engage with the various doctrines within Calvinism. I conclude with a summary of the material and an explanation for why I am neither Catholic nor Protestant. I am a Christian and a Christian alone.

SECTION ONE

Agreement and Disagreement
with Catholicism

2

The Oneness of the Church

In fairness to the Catholic readers of this work, the Protestant movement that erupted in the sixteenth century gets two things fundamentally wrong. First, Protestants clearly do not believe that there is one true, united body of Christ. This is made clear by using the term "denomination" to describe Protestant sects. To "denominate" is to divide. For example, in a math equation, the "denominator" is the figure by which the other number is divided. If a religious movement claims outright to be a "denomination," that movement is not and cannot be the one true, united body of Jesus Christ.

Scripture states that there is "one Lord, one faith, one baptism" (Eph 4:5). Unity of the body is a divine imperative. In a religious landscape fragmented by theological pluralism, the New Testament presents a picture of singularity, cohesion, and unity within the body of Christ—the church (Col 1:18).

The clearest articulation of the oneness of the body of Christ is found in Eph 4:4–6. Paul writes, "There is one body and one Spirit—just as you were called to the one hope that belongs to your call—one Lord, one faith, one baptism, one God and Father of all." Paul's sevenfold declaration of unity centers on the "one body," which is identified in Eph 1:22–23 as the church: "And he put all things under his feet and gave him as head over all things to the church, which is his body." This concept is not isolated. First Corinthians 12:12–27 expands upon the intended unity of the church by providing a metaphorical framework in which the church compares to a human body composed of many parts with differing functions, yet unified in purpose and identity. Paul declares, "For just as the body is one and has many members . . . so it is with Christ" (v. 12). All members of the body are essential, interdependent, and organically connected to one another in Christ, though each member has various gifts and functions that do not overlap with the others. To use Paul's metaphor, a body without a right arm is an incomplete body. However, the right arm does not perform the same function as the left foot. While the arm is necessary for a complete body, it would be absurd to ask the right arm to walk. That task belongs to the foot.

Jesus's high priestly prayer in John 17:20–23 provides a theological backdrop to Paul's teachings. Jesus prayed that his followers "may all be one, just as you, Father, are in me, and I in you, that they also may be in us, so that the world may believe that you have sent me" (John 17:21). The oneness of believers is rooted in the oneness of the Godhead—Father, Son, and Spirit. At his ascension, Jesus told his disciples, "Go therefore and make disciples of all nations, baptizing them in the name of the Father and of the Son and of the Holy Spirit, teaching them to observe all that I have commanded you. And behold, I am with you always, to the end of the age" (Matt 28:19–20). The term "name" in v. 19 is singular in both Greek (*onoma*) and here in English. The Father, Son, and Spirit are not three separate names but three components of the one name of God (cf. Deut 6:4). Because God is one and the Father is in the Son and the Son is in the Father (John 10:30), unity is essential.

The oneness of the body implies exclusivity and inclusivity. The "one body" of Christ can only refer to the one true church established by Christ. As such, any division within the body is not simply unfortunate but sinful. Paul's rebuke of factionalism in Corinth (cf. 1 Cor 1:10–13) underscores the theological impossibility of a fragmented body of Christ. This conviction leads to the ecclesiological conclusion that all saved persons are added to the one body of Christ by God (cf. Acts 2:47). The church is not an organization of voluntary association such as a country club or fraternity but a spiritual reality into which one enters by faith, repentance, confession, and baptism (cf. Rom 6:1–5; Gal 3:26–27). The same process that unites believers to Christ also unites them to one another.

Theologically, the body is united by a shared indwelling of the Holy Spirit. Paul states in 1 Cor 12:13, "For in one Spirit we were all baptized into one body," and again in 1 Cor 3:16, "Do you not know that you are God's temple and that God's Spirit dwells in you?" In 1 Cor 3:16, the term "you"

(Greek *humin*) is plural. Though debated, this seems to refer to the church community composed of individuals. Being baptized in one Spirit does not refer to a second experience of a so-called "Holy Spirit baptism" but to the moment of conversion and baptism into Christ. The Spirit is the means of providing the bond of unity (cf. Eph 4:3).

Denominationalism is a tragic departure from the New Testament ideal. It is true that creeds, religious hierarchies, and confessions of doctrinal allegiance have divided the Christian world. The unity of the body of Christ is often obscured by human tradition, cultural preference, and theological error. When Christians divide over nonessential matters or elevate human opinions to the level of divine law, they undermine the unity for which Christ prayed and Paul labored. The call to Christian unity does not imply a compromise of the truth. True unity must be based on the headship of Jesus Christ, his teachings, and the authority of apostolic doctrine (cf. Acts 2:42). Any ecumenical effort that bypasses or ignores doctrinal fidelity cannot achieve the unity envisioned in by Christ, the apostles, or the text of the New Testament.

If the church is one body, then its members must live in ways that reflect that reality by tangibly expressing mutual love (John 13:34–35), humility (Phil 2:1–5), and service (Rom 12:3–8). Paul's exhortation in Col 3:12–15 to "put on love, which binds everything together in perfect harmony" suggests that unity is both a divine gift and a human responsibility. Practically, this may begin by rejecting a spirit of alliance to teachers rather than to the true teaching of Scripture. Christians should refuse to elevate one teacher over another (cf. 1 Cor 3:4–7). Racial, economic, and cultural differences must be subordinated to the greater reality of union in Christ (cf. Gal 3:28). Local congregations should avoid divisive speech.

The Lord's Supper best resembles the church's shared participation in Christ (cf. 1 Cor 10:16–17) by promoting Christian unity physically, spiritually, and theologically. Physically, it brings believers together in one place, around one table, to share a common meal that proclaims the death of Christ (1 Cor 11:17–34). Spiritually, it reminds participants of their shared union with Christ and with one another through one body and one Spirit (1 Cor 10:16–17). Theologically, it reaffirms the core truths of the gospel (1 Cor 15:1–11). Christ is the atoning sacrifice (1 John 2:1–2) and thus instituted the new covenant in his blood (Jer 31:31; Luke 22:20). Christians have hope of his return. In this way, the Lord's Supper should transcend divisive boundaries by uniting believers in worship and self-examination before the cross of Jesus. When properly observed, it silences pride, heals our division, and recenters the church on the grace that makes all one in Christ.

The oneness of the body of Christ also points forward to the eschaton (i.e., the end of time). In the consummation of all things, Christ will present his church "without spot or wrinkle" (cf. Eph 5:27). This unified bride awaits her bridegroom (Rev 21:2). There will be no division in the age to come. Even so, Christ will sift his church to accept only those who truly belong to him. In Matt 25:31–46, Jesus speaks of the judgment scene in which he separates the sheep from the goats. These all stand before Jesus in the judgment having been commissioned by him to do good works for the church (cf. Matt 25:40). Here, the "goats" are not "unsaved sinners." They looked, acted, and presented themselves like true followers of Christ; yet, Christ knows their hearts. A similar event is seen in Matt 13:24–30 where Jesus tells a parable of the harvest of the wheat and the weeds. At the harvest, the two will be harvested together, then the weeds will be cast into the fire. Though they look the same, the farmer knows what is truly wheat and what only looks like wheat. The heavenly reality of the church is that only those who are truly in Christ will take on the role as his bride.

Unity is a missional imperative. Jesus explicitly connects unity with evangelistic effectiveness (cf. John 17:21). A fractured church cannot credibly proclaim a unified gospel. When the church embodies unity, it displays the reconciling power of the cross and the cosmic plan of God "to unite all things in him" (cf. Eph 1:10). Thus, the oneness of the body is a missional strategy. The true church participates in the divine agenda to gather all of God's people into one flock under the Good Shepherd (cf. John 10:16).

IS THERE DOCTRINAL UNITY WITHIN THE CATHOLIC CHURCH?

The Catholic Church, with over a billion adherents worldwide, presents itself as a bastion of unity under the leadership of the pope. However, within this seemingly unified body exist deep and long-standing doctrinal divisions. These tensions reflect real and consequential debates over theology, liturgy, ecclesial authority, and moral teaching. At the heart of many doctrinal divisions within Catholicism lies a debate over authority—both its source and its interpretation. The Church traditionally asserts a threefold foundation of authority: Scripture, Tradition, and the magisterium (i.e., the teaching office of the Church, centered primarily with the pope and the bishops). While this framework remains officially intact, divergent interpretations within these spheres generate tension.

One point of division is the role of the pope, especially in light of the doctrine of papal infallibility defined at the First Vatican Council in 1870. Some Catholics, often labeled as "traditionalists," uphold a maximalist view of papal authority, regarding the pope as the ultimate arbiter of all doctrinal matters. Others, especially in the theological left wing of Catholicism, advocate for a more collegial or conciliar model of authority. These debates intensified during the pontificates of Popes John Paul II, Benedict XVI, and Francis as each took different approaches to centralization and doctrinal enforcement.

Pope Francis's more pastoral and decentralized model of leadership has particularly exposed underlying tensions. His 2016 apostolic exhortation *Amoris Laetitia*, which opens the door to divorced and civilly remarried Catholics receiving communion under certain conditions, sparked a global debate. Some bishops' conferences embraced the interpretation, while others rejected it outright, leading to a "de facto doctrinal pluralism" within the Church.

The Second Vatican Council (1962–65) ushered in major liturgical reforms including the celebration of the Mass in vernacular languages rather than in Latin alone and a new emphasis on active lay participation and not led only by priests and other ordained figures. While these reforms were broadly accepted at the time, they later became flash points for division.

A growing movement of "traditionalist" Catholics has resisted or outright rejected the liturgical changes initiated by *Sacrosanctum Concilium* (i.e., the Vatican II document on the liturgy). Many within this movement advocate for the continued or exclusive use of the Tridentine Mass (also known as the Extraordinary Form), which was the standard form of the Roman Rite prior to 1970. These Catholics argue that the post-Vatican-II liturgy—the *Novus Ordo Missae*—lacks the theological depth, reverence, and doctrinal clarity of the old rite. In 2007, Pope Benedict XVI attempted to accommodate traditionalists by issuing *Summorum Pontificum*, which liberalized the use of the Tridentine Mass. However, Pope Francis reversed this direction in 2021 with *Traditionis Custodes*, restricting the celebration of the older liturgy. The backlash from many bishops, priests, and laypeople revealed deep fractures in the Church's understanding of liturgical identity. To traditionalists, the suppression of the old Mass represents an erasure of legitimate Catholic heritage. To reformists, resistance to liturgical change signals a dangerous rejection of conciliar authority.

Another area of division concerns Catholic moral teaching on sexual ethics. The Church's official teaching in the Catechism prohibits artificial contraception, same-sex marriage, and any sexual activity outside of heterosexual marriage. However, these teachings are increasingly challenged from within. The encyclical *Humanae Vitae* (1968), which reaffirmed the Church's opposition to artificial birth control, was met with open dissent by many theologians and laity. Over the decades, this dissent has become more widespread. Surveys routinely show that most practicing Catholics ignore or reject the Church's ban on contraception. Similarly, issues surrounding homosexuality have created significant tensions. While Catholicism distinguishes between homosexual inclination (which it does not consider sinful) and homosexual acts (which it does consider sinful), many Catholics find this distinction inadequate or harmful. Pope Francis's more pastoral tone—exemplified in his statement "Who am I to judge?"—has led some to hope for doctrinal change while others insist on the unchangeable nature of the Church's moral teachings.

Recent debates over the blessing of same-sex couples have exposed these divisions dramatically. In 2021, the Congregation for the Doctrine of the Faith reiterated that the Catholic Church cannot bless same-sex unions even while affirming the dignity of gay persons. Yet, some bishops in Germany and Belgium have openly defied this directive, conducting blessing ceremonies for same-sex couples.[1] The Vatican's apparent unwillingness to discipline these bishops underscores the fragmented nature of contemporary Catholic moral theology.

Closely related to debates about authority and reform is the issue of how the Catholic Church understands the role of women. Although Catholicism officially teaches that it lacks the authority to ordain women as priests (a position reaffirmed by John Paul II in *Ordinatio Sacerdotalis*), there remains an active debate about expanding the roles of women in ecclesial leadership. This was a primary issue in naming the pope Leo XIV after the death of Pope Francis. Advocates for reform push particularly for the female diaconate. Several commissions under recent popes have studied the question, but no decisive action has been taken. At the same time, others argue that even ordaining women as deacons would open the door to female priesthood—a prospect that traditionalists view as incompatible

---

1. Wimmer, "Bishops in Belgium."

with Catholicism's theology. The Synod on Synodality, initiated by Pope Francis in 2021, further opened these questions. While the Vatican insists that the Synod is not a legislative body, the mere airing of these issues has heightened concerns among more conservative Catholics about potential doctrinal shifts.

Underlying these issues is a broader tension between tradition and modernity. The Catholic Church faces the challenge of maintaining doctrinal continuity while engaging a rapidly changing cultural and intellectual environment. This dynamic has led to the development of opposing camps often characterized as "progressive" and "traditionalist." Progressive Catholics argue that Catholicism must adapt its doctrinal expressions to the contemporary human experience. They often draw inspiration from the ressourcement and aggiornamento themes of Vatican II, which advocate for a "living tradition" that can evolve.

On the other hand, traditionalist Catholics stress continuity with Catholicism's past practices. They view recent innovations—whether liturgical, moral, or structural—as departures from the apostolic faith. Some go as far as to question the legitimacy of the Second Vatican Council or to claim that certain post-conciliar teachings contradict previous magisterial declarations. This broader fault line has manifested in disputes over catechesis, seminary formation, ecclesial discipline, and the interpretation of papal documents. While both sides claim fidelity to Christ and to the apostolic tradition, their visions for Catholicism's future are often irreconcilable.

DIVISIONS WITHIN CATHOLIC ORDERS

The Catholic Church encompasses a wide array of religious orders, each with distinct theological emphases and doctrinal orientations. While all religious orders operate within the broader bounds of Catholic orthodoxy and loyalty to the papacy, internal diversity reflects different understandings of mission, theological method, ecclesial priorities, and the Christian life. From the scholastic rigors of the Dominicans to the mysticism of the Carmelites, and the missionary zeal of the Jesuits to the rigid reformism of the Franciscans, these orders have historically contributed to doctrinal disagreement.

Among the most significant theological divisions in Catholic history is the contrast between the Dominicans and the Franciscans—two minimalist orders that rose to prominence in the thirteenth century. The Dominicans, founded by St. Dominic de Guzmán, developed a theological tradition which emphasizes the harmony of faith and reason best exemplified in the work of St. Thomas Aquinas. As a Dominican friar, Aquinas devoted his life to the systematic study of theology and philosophy. Aquinas integrated Aristotelian logic with Christian doctrine most notably in his *Summa Theologiae*. Aquinas's theology affirms the intelligibility of truth and the Catholic Church's magisterial authority, which promoted the Dominican mission to combat heresy. His influence solidified the Dominican reputation as Catholicism's premier theological order and continues to shape Catholic intellectual tradition. Dominican theology tends to be systematic, rooted in Aristotelian philosophy, and heavily engaged with questions of natural law, metaphysics, and doctrinal precision.

In contrast, the Franciscans, founded by St. Francis of Assisi, promoted a spirituality centered on poverty, humility, and an experiential encounter with Christ. Their theological tradition shaped by figures like St. Bonaventure and John Duns Scotus leans toward a more mystical and emotional theology. John Duns Scotus's emphasis on the primacy of the will over the intellect and his defense of the Immaculate Conception distinguished Franciscan thought from the more rationalist Dominican school.

These differences led to centuries of theological rivalry. While both orders affirmed Catholic dogma, they often diverged in their explanations of doctrines such as grace, predestination, and the nature of Christ's atonement. Even today, Dominican Thomism remains the favored theological system in many seminaries and in Vatican documents. On the other hand, Franciscan theology continues to influence Catholic spirituality and Mariology.

The Society of Jesus, or the Jesuits, founded in the sixteenth century by St. Ignatius of Loyola as a response to emerging Protestant movements, introduced a new model of religious life that emphasized direct engagement with culture and politics. Jesuit theology is often characterized by its doctrinal flexibility. Rather than promoting a singular theological school, Jesuits have been known for their wide-ranging intellectual pursuits and their commitment to finding God in all things. Jesuit theologians, such as Francisco Suárez and Karl Rahner, have contributed to both scholastic and modern theological developments. Suárez, for example, advanced a version of Thomism that diverged from Dominican interpretations, namely in debates over grace and free will. In the twentieth century, Rahner's transcendental theology influenced Vatican II and post-conciliar Catholic thought.

Doctrinal tensions have occasionally arisen between the Jesuits and more traditionalist elements of the Church. Their openness to enculturation, theological pluralism, and social justice initiatives has drawn criticism from those who view them as compromising on doctrine. For instance, the Jesuits' engagement with liberation theology in Latin America was viewed with suspicion by the Vatican in the 1980s. More recently, Jesuit leadership in pushing for dialogue around issues of sexuality and ecclesial reform under Pope Francis (himself a Jesuit) has again raised eyebrows among more conservative Catholics.

The Benedictine and Carmelite traditions highlight a different axis of theological distinction. The Benedictines, among the oldest religious orders in Catholicism, follow the *Rule of St. Benedict*, which denotes a balanced life of prayer and work (noted by their motto *ora et labora*, i.e., "pray and work") and community living. Theological reflection within Benedictine monasticism tends to be liturgical, patristic, and focused on tradition. By contrast, the Carmelite Order, particularly its Discalced Reform founded by St. Teresa of Ávila and St. John of the Cross, centers on internal contemplation and mystical union with God. Carmelite theology prioritizes experiential knowledge of God over the intellect. This has contributed significantly to Catholicism's understanding of mysticism. While not prone to open doctrinal conflict, these two orders represent contrasting visions of the Christian life—one grounded in community, order, and sacred tradition; the other in solitude, asceticism, and the direct encounter with the divine.

A further source of division among religious orders lies in their relationship to Catholic reform and authority. Throughout history, certain orders have aligned themselves with reformist agendas while others have served as defenders of orthodoxy. For example, the Capuchins, a reform branch of the Franciscans, sought to restore the original ideals of Franciscan poverty in response to perceived laxity. They played a significant role in the Counter-Reformation by endorsing rigorous preaching and ethical revitalization. Similarly, the Theatines and Oratorians, smaller reform-oriented orders, were instrumental in purifying the clergy and catechizing the laity.

Conversely, some modern religious congregations, such as the Maryknoll Fathers or the Missionaries of the Sacred Heart, have emphasized social action and fellowship with non-Christian religions. These emphases have at times led to doctrinal ambiguity and internal conflict over loyalty to the teaching of the magisterium. The tension between activism and orthodoxy persists today particularly as orders grapple with how to respond to secularization, sexual ethics, and evolving cultural norms.

The Congregation for the Doctrine of the Faith has occasionally intervened when theological opinions within orders veer toward heterodoxy or heresy. In recent decades, religious orders have faced Vatican investigations over various issues. Moreover, the theological orientation of an order can affect how its members interpret doctrine in practice. For example, a Jesuit and a Dominican may both affirm the doctrine of the Trinity, but their explanations, pedagogies, and applications of that doctrine could differ significantly based on their respective traditions.

Doctrinal divisions within the Catholic Church are not new, but they have taken on renewed intensity in the modern era. While Catholicism remains united under a common hierarchy and sacramental structure, it is increasingly fragmented in its theological understanding and liturgical practice. Whether this internal pluralism will lead to further decentralization, reform, or rupture remains to be seen.

One must be fair, however, to factions within Protestant movements. Protestants have multiple denominations to be sure, and even within these denominations exist further divisions. For example, the term "Baptist" means virtually nothing today. Is one Southern Baptist, Free Will Baptist, Independent Baptist, or Reformed Baptist? Who knows? Even in these subgroups are deeper groups reflecting the political and religious spectrum of conservative and progressive.[2] Unfortunately, differences of opinion all too often override the truth of Scripture.

ONE TRUE UNDIVIDED CHURCH

The New Testament teaches that Jesus established a singular, unified body of believers. Passages such as Matt 16:18, where Jesus says, "Upon this rock I will build my church," use the singular "church," indicating a single, divinely founded institution. Similarly, Eph 4:4–6 states, "There is one body and one Spirit . . . one Lord, one faith, one baptism," affirming the early church's unity under one Lordship and one organizational structure. The "one body" referenced throughout Paul's Epistles (e.g., Rom 12:4–5; 1 Cor 12:12–13) refers to the universal church that Christ established. The body of Christ, therefore, is the original church established in the first century. Members of

---

2. For example, a schism occurred within the United Methodist denomination over the ordination of women and the inclusion of LGBTQIA+ clergy.

this body should hold that creeds and denominational schisms have led to division and even apostasy.

The existence of multiple, doctrinally conflicting sects within the Christian faith is contrary to the will of Christ. John 17:20–23 records Jesus's prayer for his followers to be one, just as he and the Father are one. This conviction must lead to a form of ecclesial exclusivism, the belief that the true church is not simply any body of believers who profess faith in Christ but specifically those who follow the pattern of New Testament Christianity. The belief in one true church reinforces the importance of scriptural authority and personal responsibility in obeying the gospel of Christ. It also upholds a view of the church as a divinely ordained body that exists for God's glory and humanity's salvation.

CONCLUSION

I agree with the Roman Catholic teaching that only one true church exists, and that this church is the body of Christ. The oneness of the church underscores the unity and mission of the New Testament church. This unity is rooted in shared faith, practice, and identity in Christ. In a religious world riven by division (not least within Catholic and Protestant movements), Christians must model the unity of the triune God, for only in such unity can the church be what it was meant to be—the one body of Christ, through whom God makes his manifold wisdom known to the world (cf. Eph 3:10). Though skewed by its own divisions, I can agree with my Catholic friends on the existence of one true church. But is the Roman Catholic Church the one true church?

3

The Universality of the Church

THE CHURCH IS A universal body open to all people regardless of ethnicity, nationality, socioeconomic status, or background. This universality reflects the scope of the inclusive nature of the gospel. From its inception in the first century, the church has embodied God's desire to redeem all of humanity through the blood of Christ. This chapter explores the theological foundation of the church's universality and examines the essential prerequisites for inclusion—faith in Jesus Christ, baptism for the forgiveness of sin, and a life of continued obedience. Together, these elements reveal the openness of the church and the seriousness of its covenantal identity.

The Bible consistently presents God's plan of salvation as inclusive and expansive. Though the Old Testament covenant was made with the people of Israel, God's promises always had a wider aim. God told Abraham, "In you all the families of the earth shall be blessed" (Gen 12:3). The prophets envisioned a day when "many peoples and strong nations shall come to seek the Lord of hosts in Jerusalem" (Zech 8:22). Further, Israel was to be a light to the nations (Isa 49:6). These early glimpses pointed toward the establishment of a new covenant (Jer 31) not based on ethnicity or birthright but on grace accessed through the Messiah.

Jesus Christ fulfilled these promises by breaking down the barriers that separated Jew from gentile. Paul proclaimed that Christ "has made us both [Jew and gentile] one and has broken down in his flesh the dividing wall of hostility" (Eph 2:14). The Great Commission reflects this universal

The Universality of the Church

vision: "Go therefore and make disciples of all nations" (Matt 28:19). This worldwide invitation marks the church as the most inclusive institution in human history. The events of Pentecost in Acts 2 confirm this reality. People "from every nation under heaven" heard the gospel in their own languages (Acts 2:5). That day, three thousand people were added to the church (Acts 2:41), forming a diverse group united by faith in the risen Christ and baptism into his body (Acts 2:38). This moment marks the beginning of a singular, global church that transcends cultural, linguistic, and geographic boundaries.

Though the church is open to whosoever will (John 3:16), entrance requires faith in Jesus Christ. Faith is not an act of intellectual assent but is active trust in Jesus as Lord and Savior. The New Testament presents faith as the first step in responding to the gospel. Paul emphasizes that we are "justified by faith apart from the works of the law" (Rom 3:28). Faith is the foundation of our covenant with Christ. It involves belief in the truth of the gospel, trust in the promises of God, and submission to the Lordship of Christ. Hebrews 11 underscores the nature of faith as a conviction that leads to action. Each figure mentioned in Heb 11 acted in accordance with God's will. Noah built, Abraham went, Moses led, etc.

Entrance into the universal church comes through belief in the identity and work of Jesus. While the invitation is extended to all, the response of faith is essential for becoming a member of the church. To be sure, the term "universal" does not refer to the belief that anyone who believes in God will be saved. In fact, Jesus said, "Not everyone who says to me, 'Lord, Lord,' will enter the kingdom of heaven, but the one who does the will of my Father who is in heaven" (Matt 7:21). In the same vein, the "universal" church does not refer to the idea that all people will go to heaven regardless of their lifestyle or acceptance of the gospel. The New Testament clearly teaches that those who are unholy, sinful, and not part of the body of Christ will be recipients of divine punishment (1 Thess 1:5–10; Rev 20:15; 21:8).

Faith alone is not enough to gain entrance into the church. James writes that even the demons believe and shudder (Jas 2:19). Further, Paul writes, "For as many of you have been baptized into Christ have put on Christ" (Gal 3:27). To gain entrance into the body of Christ, one must put him on. One does so, according to Paul, through baptism. The New Testament presents baptism as the decisive moment when one is united with Christ. On Pentecost, when the crowd asked what they must do, Peter replied, "Repent and be baptized every one of you in the name of Jesus

Christ for the forgiveness of your sins" (Acts 2:38). Those who received the word were baptized, and "there were added that day about three thousand souls" (Acts 2:41). Paul further teaches that baptism is the moment in which we are buried with Christ and raised to walk in newness of life (Rom 6:3–4). After stating that one enters Christ by being baptized into his body (Gal 3:27), Paul writes in v. 28, "There is neither Jew nor Greek, there is neither slave nor free, there is no male and female, for you are all one in Christ Jesus." Paul's words here directly link baptism with the universality of the church. Regardless of one's physical identity, baptism into Christ unites believers in him.

It is also significant that baptism is commanded universally. Jesus's words at his ascension in Matt 28:19–20 call for all disciples to be baptized. As the gospel message permeated from the Jewish context of Pentecost to the gentile world, Peter commanded Cornelius and his household to be baptized after hearing the gospel (Acts 10:48). Baptism plays a central role in every recorded conversion in Acts. Therefore, while faith opens the heart to God, baptism seals the covenant and marks the believer's entry into the church.

To this point in the discussion, I agree with the Catholic teaching that there is one universal church. I also agree that once in the church, one can lose his salvific status if he does not keep in obedience to the word and will of God. This places me in a sharp schism with my Calvinistic friends who suggest (1) a follower of Christ cannot lose his salvation or (2) if a follower of Christ is not behaving like one should, he was never truly "saved." However, Heb 6:4–6 presents one of the strongest scriptural arguments against this Calvinistic doctrine. The passage describes individuals who "have once been enlightened, who have tasted the heavenly gift, and have shared in the Holy Spirit," clearly indicating genuine believers. It then warns that if such individuals "fall away," it is impossible to renew them again to repentance, since they are "crucifying once again the Son of God to their own harm and holding him up to contempt." This warning demonstrates that it is possible for a true Christian to abandon the faith and fall beyond recovery. The language does not suggest a hypothetical situation. Hebrews 6 emphasizes the necessity of perseverance and warns against complacency in the Christian life.

Obedience is required for remaining within the church. Jesus said, "If you love me, you will keep my commandments" (John 14:15). Even the term "disciples" denotes people who are committed to following Jesus. Obedience does not earn salvation but demonstrates its reality. James writes that "faith without works is dead" (Jas 2:26), and John insists that "whoever says

'I know him' but does not keep his commandments is a liar" (1 John 2:4). The universal church must be characterized by "walking in the light as he is in the light" (1 John 1:7). This call to obedience applies equally to all. Just as salvation is offered to all, the expectation of holiness is required of all.

Understanding the church's universality has implications for evangelism, fellowship, and discipleship. First, it means that the gospel should be preached without prejudice or partiality. Christians must resist any tendency toward ethnic exclusivity or cultural favoritism. All are welcome, and none are to be turned away due to race, class, gender, or past sins. Second, fellowship among believers should reflect this unity. Paul scolded Peter for withdrawing from gentile Christians in Antioch (cf. Gal 2:11–14), insisting that such actions deny the truth of the gospel. Today, the church must reject divisions that have no basis in Scripture. Finally, the church's universality reminds believers of their identity as part of a global family. The same faith that binds American Christians also unites believers in Africa, Asia, Europe, and beyond. The universal church calls all believers to a mutual love, shared mission, and holy living.

ROMAN CATHOLIC UNIVERSALITY?

The concept of the "universal church" in Scripture refers to the spiritual body of Christ composed of all believers who have submitted to the gospel through faith, baptism, and obedience. This church is not confined to a single denomination, hierarchy, or geographical location. While the Roman Catholic Church claims to be the one true and universal church established by Christ, a careful examination of Scripture reveals significant departures in doctrine, structure, and authority. This section will argue that the Roman Catholic Church cannot be the universal church discussed in the New Testament due to (1) its hierarchical structure centered on the papacy, (2) its extrabiblical doctrines and practices, and (3) its departure from the original gospel message.

I will discuss issues concerning the papacy in a later chapter. Suffice it here to say that this system of leadership is foreign to the New Testament. In Scripture, Christ is the head of the church (Eph 1:22–23), and no single human is ever described as having universal authority over all Christians. Instead, congregations were led by a plurality of elders (also called overseers or bishops) and deacons (Phil 1:1; Acts 14:23; Titus 1:5; 1 Tim 3:1–7).

Section One

The Roman Catholic Church, with its pope and hierarchical system, does not reflect the Christ-centered structure of the New Testament church.

Another reason the Roman Catholic Church cannot be the universal church described in Scripture is its reliance on doctrines and practices that are not found in the Bible. The New Testament repeatedly emphasizes the sufficiency and finality of the apostolic teaching (cf. 2 Tim 3:16–17; Jude 3). Yet, Catholicism has added numerous teachings that go beyond or contradict Scripture. Examples would include the veneration of Mary, the belief in purgatory, the doctrine of transubstantiation, and the invocation of saints. To be sure, the New Testament honors Mary as the mother of Jesus but never portrays her as a mediator between God and man. Scripture declares that "there is one mediator between God and men, the man Christ Jesus" (1 Tim 2:5). Yet, Catholic teaching assigns Mary titles like "Co-Redemptrix" and "Queen of Heaven," and encourages the faithful to pray to her. These practices will be discussed in following chapters.

The Catholic doctrine of purgatory contradicts the clear biblical teaching that the eternal destiny of the soul is fixed at death (cf. Luke 16:19–31; Heb 9:27). The Bible does not teach a place of postmortem purification for the saved. Salvation is by grace through faith (Eph 2:8–9) offered by the blood of Jesus in baptism (Acts 22:16; 1 Pet 3:21).

Finally, the Roman Catholic Church alters the gospel by making salvation dependent on adherence to sacraments prescribed by the Church such as penance, confirmation, Eucharist, last rites, and confession, each administered by clergy who act as necessary mediators of grace. Paul's Letter to the Galatians warns against any gospel that adds to the truth of salvation by the blood of Jesus. He writes, "If anyone is preaching to you a gospel contrary to the one you received, let him be accursed" (Gal 1:9). The addition of human works, indulgences, and sacramental rituals distorts the message of the cross and undermines the sufficiency of Christ's atonement. Moreover, the Catholic Church's teaching that the Church itself is the channel through which salvation flows places undue emphasis on the institution rather than on Christ. In the New Testament, the church is not the dispenser of salvation but is the community of the saved. Christ alone saves; the church is his body, not his replacement.

The universal church mentioned in Scripture is a spiritual body composed of all who have responded to the gospel through faith, baptism, and obedience. It is governed not by a pope but by the living Christ. It adheres to the Scriptures as the sole and final authority in matters of faith and practice.

Therefore, the Roman Catholic Church cannot rightly be identified as the universal church described in the Bible.

IS THERE A UNIVERSAL CHURCH TODAY?

The ideal of one universal church—a single, united body of believers across the globe—has long been a topic of theological and ecclesiastical interest. In the New Testament, the universal church (*ekklesia*) is the body of Christ made up of all who have been saved through faith, baptism, and obedience to the gospel. The fragmentation of modern Christianity into thousands of denominations stands in stark contrast to this biblical vision of unity. So, what would it take for a truly universal church to exist today based on New Testament principles? Does such a church exist not by name or structure but in spiritual reality among those who faithfully follow Christ?

The New Testament lays out clear principles that define what the universal church is and who belongs to it. These criteria include (1) submission to the authority of Christ, (2) adherence to the gospel, (3) faith and baptism, and (4) ongoing obedience and holiness.

First, the universal church must recognize and submit to Jesus Christ as its sole head. Paul declares, "[God] gave him as head over all things to the church, which is his body" (Eph 1:22-23). Any church that elevates human authority—whether pope, council, or tradition—above Christ violates this fundamental principle. The universal church today must center itself entirely on the teachings, authority, and example of Jesus.

In doing so, the church must teach the original, apostolic message found in the New Testament. Paul warned the Galatians that any deviation from the gospel he preached—whether by man or angel—was unacceptable (Gal 1:6-9). The universal church cannot be built on evolving traditions, novel revelations, or doctrinal innovations. It must teach the same gospel proclaimed by the apostles (1 Cor 15:1-4).

In Acts 2, when the church was first established, Peter declared that in response to the gospel, one must "repent and be baptized . . . for the forgiveness of sins" (Acts 2:38). Those who responded in faith were "added to their number" (v. 41). These terms—faith, repentance, and baptism—are the entrance conditions for the church. The universal church today must require the same. Baptism is not an optional symbol, but the divinely appointed means of entering Christ's body and receiving forgiveness of sins

(Rom 6:3–4; Gal 3:27). Faith without baptism, or baptism without faith, does not satisfy the pattern laid down in Scripture.

The church is a community of disciples. Jesus commanded his followers to "teach them to observe all that I have commanded you" (Matt 28:20). The universal church is holy, set apart from the world (1 Pet 2:9) and marked by a life of ongoing obedience. Doctrinal purity and moral integrity are not negotiable. Churches that tolerate immorality, false teaching, or compromise with the world cannot represent the true, universal church of Jesus Christ.

What would it take for such a church to exist today? First, there must be the rejection of denominational division. Denominations exist because of theological, doctrinal, and often cultural divisions. Yet Paul writes, "Is Christ divided?" (1 Cor 1:13). The proliferation of denominations undermines the unity that Jesus prayed for in John 17:21. The universal church would require believers to lay aside sectarian identities and unite solely under the name of Christ.

Additionally, there must be a return to the Bible alone as the sole authority in the church. Many Christian congregations base their teachings on creeds, confessions, or traditions that supplement or even override Scripture. The universal church must return to the Bible as the sole authority in matters of faith and practice. This means restoring the simple and powerful gospel of the New Testament.

The New Testament church grew by faithful preaching. The universal church would need to recover this mission-minded focus. Evangelism must be coupled with discipleship, thereby ensuring that converts are not only baptized but are taught to live in obedience to Christ. Does a universal church exist today? If we define the universal church as a human institution or denominational sect, the answer is no. No organization today fully embodies all the traits of the New Testament church without error or compromise. However, if we define the universal church as the spiritual body of Christ composed of all people who have obeyed the gospel—believing, repenting, being baptized, and continuing in faithful obedience—then yes, the universal church does exist. It exists wherever people have been born again of water and the Spirit (John 3:5). It exists wherever disciples worship in the appropriate manner that is prescribed and described in Scripture and by worshiping in spirit and truth (John 4:24). It may be scattered across house churches, mission fields, or faithful congregations. Nevertheless, it exists because God himself is still adding obedient souls to his church (Acts 2:47).

The Universality of the Church

The challenge for believers today is not to create a new universal church, but to restore and recognize the one Jesus already built by returning to the pattern of the New Testament. Unity will come not by negotiation, but by submission to the Word of God. In this sense, we must strive to fulfill the mission of the universal church by adhering closely to the New Testament pattern for doctrine, worship, and Christian living. Our plea must be to "speak where the Bible speaks and be silent where the Bible is silent." We must reject denominational creeds, human traditions, and centralized church governance, and instead maintain autonomous congregations overseen by qualified elders (Titus 1:5–9; 1 Tim 3:1–7) as it was in the first-century church. Our teaching on salvation must reflect the New Testament model of faith in Jesus Christ (Heb 11:6), repentance of sins (Acts 17:30), confession that Christ is Lord (Matt 16:16; Rom 10:9–10), and baptism by immersion for the forgiveness of sins (Acts 2:38; 22:16; Rom 6:3–4). This commitment to biblical teaching mirrors the structure, doctrine, and mission of the original church established by Christ and his apostles.

Moreover, we must emphasize unity by seeking to unite all believers by returning to the practices and teachings of the first-century church. Worship should be kept simple and reverent featuring congregational singing without instruments, weekly observance of the Lord's Supper, and preaching centered on Scripture (cf. Acts 20:7). Evangelism and discipleship remain central. Members are encouraged to share the gospel, support mission work, and grow in their own holiness. While not claiming perfection, we must endeavor to be simply Christians—nothing more and nothing less—thereby participating in and reflecting the universal body of Christ.

CONCLUSION

The church of Jesus Christ is universal in scope and nature. Anyone, from anywhere, may become part of it—if they respond in faith, are baptized into Christ, and live a life of obedience to him. These prerequisites do not restrict the church's reach. Rather, they preserve its holiness and covenantal identity. Some factions of Christianity are known only by their locale. For example, Cumberland Presbyterian, Coptic Christian, Russian Orthodox, and, dare I say, *Roman* Catholic. In a world fractured by division, the church stands as a living witness to the unifying power of the gospel—a family drawn from every nation, tribe, and tongue, united by one Lord, one faith, and one baptism (Eph 4:5).

4

What Did the Earliest Church Look Like?

THE FIRST TWO CENTURIES of the Christian church witnessed rapid expansion and intense persecution. In the absence of the apostles, the early Christian community faced the dual task of preserving apostolic teaching and articulating its own identity within the Greco-Roman world. This period laid the groundwork for the later ecumenical councils and ecclesiastical structures. As such, it provides a crucial lens for understanding the DNA of Christian leadership, worship, ecclesiology, and theology.

The book of Acts defines the image and practice of the early church. However, it does not take long for the religious group known as "Christians" to behave in ways contrary to apostolic teaching. When we look at Christian groups today, does one exist that patterns itself after the New Testament apostolic example? If so, what does that look like, and how do we know? Drawing upon primary sources from the Apostolic Fathers and early Christian apologists, this chapter explores how the postapostolic church preserved continuity with the apostolic message while responding to internal and external challenges. The evidence demonstrates that the early church developed a cohesive and resilient identity grounded in apostolic tradition, worship, leadership, and orthodoxy.

FROM APOSTOLIC TO EPISCOPAL AUTHORITY

In the immediate aftermath of Pentecost (Acts 2), the leadership of the church remained in the hands of the apostles who functioned as witnesses to the resurrection (cf. Acts 1:21–22). By the end of the first century, a transition was underway from apostolic authority to localized episcopal oversight. The terms "episcopal," "bishop," "pastor," "elder," and "shepherd" are used interchangeably in the New Testament to refer to a plurality of leaders in the local congregation (cf. Titus 1:5,7; Acts 14:23).

The Didache (ca. AD 70–120) reflects this transitional phase. "Appoint for yourselves bishops and deacons worthy of the Lord . . . for they also perform the ministry of the prophets and teachers" (Didache 15.1). This passage not only acknowledges the replacement of apostolic leadership after the death of the apostles but also equates bishops and deacons with the divinely commissioned roles previously established in the New Testament (cf. 1 Tim 3; Titus 1).

Ignatius of Antioch (d. 110), writing en route to martyrdom, provides the most complete early witness to the monepiscopacy, i.e., the authority of a singular leader in the church. In his Letter to the Smyrnaeans, he insists, "Wherever the bishop appears, there let the people be; as wherever Jesus Christ is, there is the Catholic Church" (Ignatius, *Smyrnaeans* 8.2). However, the phrase "the bishop" need not only refer to a singular leader but could refer to one of many. The emphasis seems to be that the bishop carries his authority outside the corporate gathering of the church. For Ignatius, ecclesial unity and orthodoxy are inseparable from episcopal authority. His repeated exhortations to submit to the bishop suggest that the office had become normative in the major Christian centers.

By the time of Irenaeus of Lyons (ca. 180), episcopal succession had become the guarantor of doctrinal fidelity. He writes, "It is within the power of all . . . to contemplate clearly the tradition of the apostles manifested throughout the whole world; and we are in a position to enumerate those who were instituted bishops by the apostles . . . and to demonstrate that they have handed down that faith" (Irenaeus, *Against Heresies* 3.3.1). Thus, by the late second century, apostolic succession was a historical claim. However, Acts 14:23 states that Paul established elders in every church. This is the apostolic institution of church leadership. These bishops/elders were placed in every congregation, implying the autonomy of congregations. The role of the plurality of leaders in the local congregation was to teach truth given to them from the apostles and to protect the church from false teaching.

Within the first two hundred years of the church, the model of leadership changed from a plurality of male-led elders to councils of bishops who oversaw multiple congregations. Finally, in AD 498, Pope Symmachus was elected to be the first pope.[1] There is no place in the New Testament that allows for any leadership other than a local plurality of men who uphold the qualities set forth in 1 Tim 3:1–7 and Titus 1:6–9.

WORSHIP: WORD, TABLE, AND THE SHAPE OF CHRISTIAN LITURGY

Worship in the early church was deeply rooted in Jewish liturgical patterns adapted to reflect the Christ-event. Justin Martyr's *First Apology* (ca. 155) provides the most detailed account of second-century Christian worship.

> On the day called Sunday, all who live in cities or in the country gather together in one place, and the memoirs of the apostles or the writings of the prophets are read. . . . Then we all rise together and pray. . . . Then bread and wine and water are brought . . . and the president likewise offers prayers and thanksgivings . . . and the people assent, saying Amen (Justin Martyr, *First Apology* 67).

This passage reveals several enduring features of Christian worship. It mentions the weekly practices of reading of Scripture, prayer, the Eucharist, and Sunday as the time of observance.

Justin identifies the Eucharist as a continuation of the Last Supper. He writes, "For not as common bread and common drink do we receive these; but . . . the food which has been made into the Eucharist . . . is both the flesh and blood of that Jesus who was made flesh" (Justin Martyr, *First Apology* 66). Ignatius similarly affirms the Eucharist as central to Christian worship, calling it "the medicine of immortality" (Ignatius, *Ephesians* 20.2).

In addition to the Eucharist, early Christian worship incorporated psalms, hymns, and spiritual songs (Eph 5:19; Col 3:16). The practice of gathering before dawn and singing "a hymn to Christ as to a god," as Pliny the Younger states in his letter to Trajan, implies that worship through song was a regular practice of the early church.[2] The early church's worship was

---

1. Hughes, *History of the Church*, 319.
2. "They asserted, however, that the sum and substance of their fault or error had

characterized by simplicity. Early Christian writers frequently emphasized vocal music—psalms, hymns, and spiritual songs—as the preferred form of worship. No allowance for mechanical instrumental worship is prescribed in the New Testament. Clement of Alexandria (ca. 150–215), for instance, encouraged believers to "employ a living lyre, our tongue," and warned against the use of "flutes and psalteries" as belonging to "the common herd" (Clement, *Paedagogus* 2.4). The use of instruments was avoided due to their association with pagan rituals and theatrical performances. This theological preference for a cappella singing became a defining feature of early Christian worship.

By the second century, while instrumental music was prominent in Roman civic and religious life, the church maintained its distance from such practices. Eusebius of Caesarea, quoting earlier sources, notes that Christian worship involved "plain song" and avoided elaborate musical displays (Eusebius, *Commentary on the Psalms*, PG 23:1172). Additionally, given the biblical theology of Christ, instruments, like the sacrificial system of the law of Moses, were seen as part of the old covenant and associated with Levitical temple worship now fulfilled and surpassed in Christ. This view persisted for centuries, with most early church fathers either silent on or critical of instrumental accompaniment in worship. The overwhelming emphasis remained on unity, edification, and intelligibility—qualities best embodied through congregational singing. Thus, the historical record indicates that for at least the first two centuries of the church's life, instrumental music was largely absent from Christian liturgical practice.

THEOLOGY: CHRISTOLOGY, SOTERIOLOGY, AND THE RULE OF FAITH

Theological reflection in the early church centered on the identity of Christ and the meaning of salvation. The earliest heresies—docetism, gnosticism, and adoptionism—forced the church to articulate a coherent Christology. Docetism taught that Jesus only seemed to have a physical body and did not truly become human or suffer physically. The term comes from the

---

been that they were accustomed to meet on a fixed day before dawn and sing responsively a hymn to Christ as to a god, and to bind themselves by oath, not to do some crime, but not to commit fraud, theft, or adultery, not falsify their trust, nor to refuse to return a trust when called upon to do so. When this was over, it was their custom to depart and to assemble again to partake of food—but ordinary and innocent food." See Pliny the Younger, *Letters* 10.96.

Greek word *dokeō* meaning "to seem" or "to appear." According to docetic belief, the incarnation, crucifixion, and resurrection of Jesus were not actual physical events but illusions or symbolic acts. Ignatius of Antioch refuted Docetism by affirming that Jesus Christ "was truly born, and did eat and drink . . . was truly crucified and died" (Ignatius, *Trallians* 9.1–2). For Ignatius, salvation required a real incarnation, real suffering, and real resurrection.

Justin Martyr presents a *logos* Christology, which identifies Jesus as the preexistent *logos* (i.e., "Word") who became incarnate (John 1:1–4). Justin writes, "The Word, who is the first-begotten of God, is also God" (*First Apology* 63). His *logos* theology allowed early Christians to present their faith as consistent with Jewish monotheism. Irenaeus, combating Gnosticism, developed a "recapitulation" theology in which Christ reverses Adam's fall. He writes, "He [Christ] recapitulated in himself the long line of the human race . . . so that he might fight for our forefathers and vanquish through Adam what had stricken us through Adam" (*Against Heresies* 3.18.1). Early Christian theology included repeated citations of the Gospels, Pauline Letters, and other apostolic writings as Scripture (e.g., 2 Clem. 2.4; Polycarp, *Philippians* 12.1).

The so-called "Rule of Faith" (*regula fidei*) functioned as a proto-creedal boundary for orthodoxy. It was a concise summary of apostolic teaching used in the early church as a standard for orthodoxy and a safeguard against heresy. While not a formal creed, the Rule of Faith functioned as a theological framework rooted in the narrative of Scripture.[3] Early Christians used it to articulate the essentials of the Christian faith such as belief in God the Father, Jesus Christ as the incarnate Son, the Holy Spirit, the church, the resurrection of the body, and eternal life. It provided a criterion for who could and could not be considered a Christian.

Church fathers frequently referenced the Rule of Faith to combat false teachings and to affirm the unity of Christian doctrine. Irenaeus wrote, "The Church, though dispersed throughout the whole world . . . has received this faith from the apostles and their disciples" (*Against Heresies* 1.10.1). He proceeded to list the basic elements of the Christian confession. This faith includes belief in one God, the Father Almighty, the Creator of heaven, earth, and all things therein; in one Christ Jesus, the Son of God, who was incarnate for our salvation; and in the Holy Spirit, who spoke through the prophets to reveal God's plan, including the coming of Christ, his virgin

---

3. Ferguson, *Rule of Faith*, xi–xii.

birth, suffering, crucifixion under Pontius Pilate, resurrection, and ascension. Furthermore, it affirms Christ's future return from heaven in glory to raise all flesh and to judge the living and the dead, granting eternal life to the righteous and eternal punishment to the wicked (*Against Heresies* 1.10.1). Similarly, Tertullian described the Rule as the faith Christians hold, "by which we believe that there is but one God . . . and that he sent his Word . . . who was born of the virgin . . . crucified . . . raised again . . . sent the Holy Spirit . . . and will come again to judge the quick and the dead" (*Prescription Against Heretics* 13). The Rule of Faith thus served as both a catechetical tool and a theological boundary marker.

CONCLUSION

From AD 33 to 200, the church developed a distinct and enduring identity marked by apostolic succession, liturgical worship, communal ecclesiology, and theological orthodoxy. The voices of the early fathers—Ignatius, Justin, Irenaeus, and others—testify to a community striving for faithfulness amid persecution and heresy. These centuries laid the essential foundations for the doctrinal cohesion of later Christian history.

When compared to the earliest church of the New Testament, one only sees worship in song without instruments, corporate worship on Sunday, emphasis on the Lord's Supper, and teaching/reading from Scripture. While much of this is done in congregations around the globe, what is not seen in the early church is a one-person leadership model nor one individual or council overseeing multiple congregations. Those are later developments that have no basis in Scripture. The Roman Catholic Church claims to be the original New Testament church in Scripture. Yet, the practice of Roman Catholicism today is very different from the practice of the first-century church.

5

Salvation in Christ and...?

THE QUESTION OF SALVATION lies at the center of Christian theology. Within Roman Catholicism, the sacraments are not merely symbolic but are efficacious signs of grace instituted by Christ and entrusted to the Church for the sanctification of believers. Catholic doctrine asserts that salvation is mediated through the Church by means of the seven sacraments: baptism, confirmation, Eucharist, penance, anointing of the sick, holy orders, and matrimony. This view presupposes an understanding of grace that is rooted in one's sacramental actions and the approval of the clergy, which contrasts sharply with the perspective of many Protestant traditions that affirm the sufficiency of Christ as the sole means of salvation. This chapter will first present a detailed overview of the sacramental system and its soteriological implications before offering a theological rebuttal grounded in a baptism-centric view of salvation.

THE CATHOLIC DOCTRINE OF THE SACRAMENTS

The CCC defines sacraments as "efficacious signs of grace, instituted by Christ and entrusted to the Church, by which divine life is dispensed to us" (CCC 1131). The sacramental system is thus the ordinary means by which salvation is applied to individuals. Catholic teaching holds that the sacraments are not mere symbols but instruments of sanctifying grace, functioning *ex opere operato* ("by the work worked") when properly administered and received.

The Catholic Church views itself as the divinely appointed steward of the sacraments. As the "universal sacrament of salvation" (Lumen Gentium §48), the Catholic Church is both the locus and the agent through which the means of grace flow. This sacramental economy is tightly bound to ecclesiology. The visible Church through apostolic succession ensures the valid administration of the sacraments. Consequently, salvation is not viewed as an individualistic experience but as a communal journey mediated by ecclesial authority.

Baptism occupies a unique place as the foundational sacrament. The CCC affirms that "baptism is necessary for salvation for those to whom the Gospel has been proclaimed and who have had the possibility of asking for this sacrament" (CCC 1257). It removes sin (Acts 22:16), incorporates the believer into the Church (Gal 3:27), and imparts sanctifying grace (1 Pet 3:21). In the Catholic tradition, baptism opens the door to the other sacraments, which deepen and preserve the grace first conferred.

The Eucharist is central to Catholic worship and theology. The doctrine of transubstantiation teaches that the bread and wine become the actual body and blood of Christ, often called the real or true presence of Christ. It is considered "the source and summit of the Christian life" (Lumen Gentium §11). This reinforces the necessity of continual sacramental participation for sustaining salvation. Participation in the Eucharist must be ongoing for one to remain in a saved state. Only those confirmed by the Catholic Church may partake of the Eucharist. I will address matters of transubstantiation in a later chapter.

Catholics argue that post-baptismal sin requires sacramental reconciliation. The Catholic Church teaches that penance restores one's relationship with God and the Church by renewing sanctifying grace. Penance is not synonymous with repentance. William Tyndale, in his English translation of the New Testament, notably rejected the Latin Vulgate's rendering of *paenitentiam agite* ("do penance") in favor of "repent." This distinction was theologically significant, as the Catholic Church's sacramental system had long equated penance with external acts of contrition prescribed by a priest. Tyndale emphasized inner repentance—a change of heart and mind—rather than performance. His translation challenged the Catholic Church's authority by highlighting the personal and spiritual nature of repentance. Penance is the act of doing good works to override one's evil deeds. Repentance, on the other hand, is the act of changing one's mind and refusing to do those sinful acts in the future. Similarly, the act of anointing of the sick claims to provide healing and the forgiveness of sins particularly at the end of life. These sacraments are necessary responses to human weakness that may occur after baptism. Confirmation completes baptismal grace, matrimony sanctifies conjugal life, and holy orders confer the grace of ministry. Each sacrament provides a specific grace that contributes to the salvation and sanctification of the individual within their vocational calling. Together, they integrate personal salvation into the life of the Church.

THE THEOLOGICAL FOUNDATIONS OF SACRAMENTAL SALVATION

The Catholic understanding of sacraments rests on a realist interpretation of grace. For the Catholic, salvation is not a forensic declaration (as in many Protestant systems) but an ontological transformation. Thus, grace is infused rather than imputed. Augustine of Hippo speaks of grace as an inward "medicine" that God "pours into" (*infundit*) the human heart, enabling the will to obey the divine law and transforming sinners into the just.[1] Thomas Aquinas adopts and refines this Augustinian notion. In the *Summa Theologiae*, he distinguishes *gratia gratum faciens* (habitual, justifying grace) from transient actual grace by describing the former as a "supernatural quality inhering in the soul" that God infuses so the person may participate in the divine nature.[2] Augustine stresses the healing of concupiscence, while Aquinas, using Aristotelian categories, explains how infused grace elevates each faculty of the soul to its proper supernatural end.

Biblical support is drawn from texts such as John 3:5 ("unless one is born of water and the Spirit"), Jas 5:14–15 (anointing the sick), and 1 Cor 11:27–29 (the gravity of eucharistic participation). The church fathers consistently upheld the efficacy of sacramental signs as means of grace. Catholicism integrates these into a coherent soteriology where salvation is both initiated and sustained through the sacraments.

---

1. Augustine, *On the Spirit* 32, 113.
2. Aquinas, *Summa Theologiae* 1–2, Q110, A2.

A REBUTTAL: BAPTISM INTO CHRIST AS SUFFICIENT FOR SALVATION

Scripture teaches that one desiring devotion to God must participate in sacramental rites. While not all sacraments prescribed by the Catholic Church are required by Scripture (e.g., marriage), baptism and the Lord's Supper are. Thus, any Christian group that does not believe in the necessity of baptism as the means by which sins are forgiven (Acts 22:16; 1 Pet 3:21) and does not take the Lord's Supper every Sunday (cf. Acts 20:7) are not participating in the rituals that maintain one's connection to Christ and status within his church.

While Catholic doctrine affirms the necessity of the sacraments, especially baptism, a theological case can be made that baptism alone is sufficient for receiving salvation. Scripture repeatedly affirms baptism as the decisive moment of salvation:

> Acts 22:16: "Now why do you wait? Rise and be baptized, washing away your sins, calling on his name!"

> Romans 6:3–4: "Do you not know that all of us who have been baptized into Christ Jesus were baptized into his death?"

> Galatians 3:27: "For as many of you as were baptized into Christ have put on Christ."

> 1 Peter 3:21: "Baptism, which corresponds to this, now saves you."

These passages indicate that baptism unites the believer with Christ's death and resurrection. Baptism is portrayed as the full entry into the saving grace of Christ. Only at baptism are one's sins forgiven, removed, and forgotten.

THE SUFFICIENCY OF CHRIST'S ATONEMENT

Hebrews 10:14 states, "By one sacrifice he has made perfect forever those who are being made holy." The notion of repeated sacramental rites to restore grace implies that Christ's atonement is insufficient apart from continual mediation. In contrast, Scripture clearly and forcefully affirms the finality and completeness of Christ's work. The believer's union with Christ through baptism is the moment of justification, regeneration, and sanctification—initiated by God's grace and received through faith. This does not imply that Christians are not called to live holy lives. Equally wrong is the popular Protestant notion of "once saved, always saved." Though not all Protestants adhere to this doctrine, many, namely in Calvinist circles, claim that because God predestined who he would save, then no one can refuse salvation and thus no one can lose salvation. However, these doctrines are also met with scriptural opposition.

John 3:16—often called the "golden text" of Scripture—states that it is "whosoever believes" that will be saved. Additionally, God sent his Son to save the world and thus does not limit Christ's saving work to a select few. In fact, if Christ only saved the elect who were already elect before the foundation of the world, why send Christ at all? Further, Heb 6 warns against the danger of falling away. In this context, falling away is marked by apostasy and blatant continual sin, not sins committed amid a desire to live in righteousness. First John 2:1 states, "My little children, I am writing these things to you so that you may not sin. But if anyone does sin, we have an advocate with the Father, Jesus Christ the righteous," implying the possibility and probability that Christians do and will sin. While the believer has assurance of salvation, that assurance is only possible "if we walk in the light as he is in the light" (1 John 1:7). If we fail to walk in the light or reject the gospel even after receiving and obeying it, we lose our salvific status (Heb 6:4–6).

The Catholic model requires sacramental mediation through ordained clergy. Yet, 1 Pet 2:9 declares that all Christians are a "royal priesthood." The necessity of clerical mediation for sacramental grace is thus called into question. Under the new covenant, the believer has direct access to God through Christ who is the sole mediator (1 Tim 2:5; Heb 9:15; 12:24).

James calls believers to confess their sins to one another (Jas 5:16). There is no mandate in Scripture for a Christian to confess his sins to a priest or to do any type of penance as a result. Forgiveness comes in the confession of sins and repentance (*metanoeō*, literally, "to change one's mind"). In this sense, the use of sacraments to receive forgiveness does not align with Scripture since there are no ordained individuals with the power to absolve sin. As a priesthood of believers, the Christian's role is to direct the sinner to Christ asking for forgiveness and bearing one another's burdens (Gal 6:15).

The repeated need for sacramental grace promoted by Catholicism undercuts the sufficiency of Christ's atonement. By contrast, a baptism-centered view in which baptism is the means by which (1) sins are washed away (Acts 22:16), (2) one joins the body of Christ (Gal 3:27), and (3) the reenactment of the death, burial, and resurrection of Christ (Rom 6:1–4) maintains the necessity of a response in obedience to the gospel and the sufficiency of Christ's once-for-all sacrifice.

CONCLUSION

Catholic theology presents the sacraments as divinely instituted means of grace necessary for salvation by framing them within an ecclesial structure that mediates Christ's presence and power. This view upholds a high view of the Church, sacramental realism, and an integrated life of grace. However, a baptism-centered rebuttal emphasizes the sufficiency of faith in Christ and the decisive nature of baptism for salvation. While not denying the value of ongoing Christian practices or the need for a repentant life, this position rejects the necessity of additional sacramental rites for attaining or maintaining salvation. At stake is the nature of grace itself—whether it is infused through institutional sacraments or received directly through union with Christ. The New Testament, when taken on its own terms, favors the latter.

Is there a Christian doctrine that teaches faithfully what the Bible says about maintaining one's salvation? Scripture does not uphold the doctrine of "once saved, always saved." To be sure, continued life in Christ is a requirement for the believer. But what does that continued life in Christ look like? First, the Christian is called to walk in the light and to walk by faith (1 John 1:7; 2 Cor 5:7). While a command to be absolved of sins from a priest is never mentioned in Scripture, forgiving others, confessing our sins to one another, and asking the Lord for forgiveness are required for the Christian.

6

The Priesthood and Papal Authority

ACCORDING TO THE CCC, the sacrament of holy orders is defined as follows:

> Holy Orders is the sacrament through which the mission entrusted by Christ to his apostles continues to be exercised in the Church until the end of time: thus it is the sacrament of apostolic ministry (CCC 1536).

This sacrament includes three degrees or orders (cf. CCC 1554): (1) the episcopate (i.e., bishops), (2) the presbyterate (i.e., the priesthood), and (3) the diaconate (i.e., deacons). The CCC further explains:

> The sacrament of Holy Orders communicates a "sacred power" which is none other than that of Christ. The exercise of this authority must therefore be measured against the model of Christ, who by love made himself the least and the servant of all (CCC 1551).

Regarding the effect of the sacrament, the CCC states:

> This sacrament configures the recipient to Christ by a special grace of the Holy Spirit, so that he may serve as Christ's instrument for his Church. By ordination one is enabled to act as a representative of Christ (CCC 1581).
>
> It is true that someone validly ordained can, for grave reasons, be discharged from the obligations and functions linked to ordination . . . but he cannot become a layman again in the strict

sense, because the character imprinted by ordination is forever (CCC 1583).

These three components form an essential part of Catholicism's ecclesial identity. "Holy orders" are understood as one of the seven sacraments through which the mission of Christ continues. The priesthood is the means by which grace is administered to the faithful, and the papacy represents the visible sign of unity and authority in the Roman church. However, when examined through the lens of Scripture, several elements of these teachings warrant reevaluation. We will find that there is absolutely no basis for the papacy in Scripture. Additionally, the offices of church leaders are limited to elders and deacons, both requiring marriage and families rather than celibacy.

HOLY ORDERS IN CATHOLIC THEOLOGY

Catholic theology emphasizes the ontological change that occurs in the recipient of holy orders. Ordination, especially to the priesthood, confers a permanent spiritual character (CCC 1582). Through this change, the ordained becomes a representative of Christ, namely in the celebration of the Eucharist, the forgiveness of sins, and the administration of the sacraments. But is such an ordination scriptural?

While the New Testament acknowledges the existence of leadership in the early church with elderships over each congregation, it does not describe a sacrament of ordination that imparts an indelible character. Acts 6 and 1 Tim 3 demonstrate the appointment of deacons and elders, but the process resembles a commissioning rather than a ritualistic ordination. Additionally, elders are instituted to their role with prayer and fasting (Acts 14:23), not by taking vows. Elders and deacons both must be married in monogamous relationships and have children (cf. 1 Tim 3:1–13). The priesthood in Catholicism requires celibacy, a notion completely contrary to Scripture. Although Scripture does speak of those who are celibate as being devoted to the church, there is no distinction between the leaders and laity in the context of 1 Cor 7:25–31.

In Heb 7:23–28, Christ is identified as the eternal High Priest, whose priesthood is unchangeable and who alone mediates between God and man (cf. 1 Tim 2:5). The New Testament model emphasizes the priesthood of all believers (1 Pet 2:9) wherein each Christian, through baptism, has direct access to God through the sacrifice of Christ. While congregational leadership is necessary and commanded by Scripture, the concept of ordination via holy orders lacks biblical precedent. Instead, elders are appointed to lead and shepherd the congregational flock, and deacons are appointed to serve the congregation's needs.

THE PRIESTHOOD IN CATHOLICISM

In Catholic teaching, the priest serves *in persona Christi*, particularly in the administration of the Eucharist where the bread and wine are believed to become the body and blood of Christ. The priest is also essential for the sacrament of reconciliation. In this way, the priest acts as a mediator who has the authority to absolve sins. This view is grounded in the belief that Jesus instituted the ministerial priesthood at the Last Supper when he commanded the apostles to "do this in remembrance of me" (Luke 22:19) and gave them authority to forgive sins (John 20:23). While Christ commissioned his apostles with unique authority (e.g., Matt 28:18–20), the New Testament presents a communal priesthood of all believers in Christ. Hebrews 10:11–14 explains that Jesus offered a single, perfect sacrifice for sins and that no repeated sacrificial offering is needed. Moreover, the practice of confessing sins to one another (Jas 5:16) and praying for one another stands in contrast to the necessity of a priestly intermediary. The New Testament teaches that access to God comes through Christ alone (Heb 4:14–16). There is no precedence in the New Testament for a Christian to approach any ordained person to have his sins forgiven. In the model prayer, Jesus plainly states, "And forgive us our debts as we also have forgiven our debtors" (Matt 6:12). Yes, we must confess, and yes, we must ask forgiveness, but not from a priest. We confess to God and to one another (1 John 1:9) and ask forgiveness from those whom we have wronged and from God.

THE PAPACY IN CATHOLICISM

The Catholic Church teaches that the pope is the successor of Peter and the visible head of the Church. This view is primarily based on Jesus's words in Matt 16:18–19, where Jesus says to Peter, "You are Peter, and on this rock I will build my church." Catholic tradition holds that Peter was given primacy among the apostles.

> The Lord made Simon alone, whom he named Peter, the "rock" of his Church. He gave him the keys of his Church and instituted him shepherd of the whole flock. The office of binding and loosing which was given to Peter was also assigned to the college of apostles united to its head. This pastoral office of Peter and the other apostles belongs to the Church's very foundation and is continued by the bishops under the primacy of the pope (CCC 881).

As such, the pope is believed to possess the charism of infallibility when he proclaims doctrines *ex cathedra* concerning faith and morals.[1] Thus, Catholicism teaches that he serves as the supreme pastor and teacher of all Christians.

Matthew 16:18–19 is often cited as the foundational text for the papacy. However, many scholars interpret the phrase "on this rock" (*epi tautē petra*) to refer not to Peter himself, but to Peter's confession of faith in Christ as the Son of God (Matt 16:16). There are a few reasons for this. First, the words *petros* and *petra* are different, even if only slightly. Jesus says, "You are *petros* and upon this *petra* I will build my church." The first term, *petros*, is masculine in Greek, which denotes a standalone boulder.[2] In this sense, Jesus's nickname to Simon, now Peter, demonstrates his strength, leadership, and loyalty. However, the second term *petra* is feminine in Greek, likely denoting a gravel bed or rock foundation.[3] Many scholars have noted the difference, but the implications of this difference are still heavily debated. On the one hand, the term could refer to Peter's confession as noted previously. This is the traditional view. According to this view, Jesus is saying that the confession that he is the Son of God will be the foundation on which the church is built. While this view has merit, it is not the first time such a confession had been uttered. In John 1:49, Nathaniel makes the same confession as do the demons in Luke 4:9. The better interpretation is that the term *petra* refers to the entire group of the apostles who were gathered with Jesus at this time. I imagine Jesus telling Peter privately, "You're the boulder," then pointing to his apostles saying, "and this *gravel bed of the apostles* will be the foundation of the church."

In either case, Peter was never placed as the one leader of the church after the ascension of Christ. In fact, the New Testament portrays a collegial leadership among the apostles (cf. Acts 15), where James, not Peter,

---

1. Vatican Council I, *Pastor Aeternus* 2, in *Decrees of the Ecumenical Councils*, 816.
2. BDAG, s.v., "Πέτρος."
3. BDAG, s.v., "πέτρα."

presides over the Jerusalem council. Further, the apostle Paul had to rebuke Peter to his face in Gal 2:11 because he "had clearly done wrong" (NET). Is this papal infallibility? Clearly not. Furthermore, just a few verses after Peter's good confession, Jesus rebukes Peter, calling him "Satan" for misunderstanding his mission (Matt 16:23). This too indicates Peter's leadership was not infallible. Additionally, Peter is never called *pater* (Greek for "father") in Scripture. Aside from being an apostle, Scripture states that Peter was a husband (which the pope is not allowed to be; cf. Mark 1:30, Luke 4:38) and an elder (1 Pet 5:1).

Perhaps the greatest issue with papal authority is that Christ alone is the head of his church now and forever. Christ is described as the head of the church in Eph 5:23 and Col 1:18. The idea of a single person presiding over the universal church developed over time and does not reflect the structure of the first-century church. It is not until the fourth century that the term *papa*—from which the English word "pope" is derived—emerges as a formal religious title, though it was used more broadly as a term of respect for bishops in general. By the late fourth and early fifth centuries, particularly in the West, it became increasingly associated with the bishop of Rome. Eventually, by the sixth century, under Pope Gregory I, the title "pope" (*papa*) became reserved exclusively for the Roman pontiff.[4]

THE BIBLE AND ECCLESIAL AUTHORITY

The sacrament of holy orders supports a hierarchical, priestly system that claims apostolic succession and magisterial authority. The early church emphasized servant leadership (Matt 23:8–12) and accountability to Christ. Authority was derived from Scripture and the indwelling of the Holy Spirit, not from any hierarchical status. Elders and deacons were appointed to serve (Acts 20:28; Phil 1:1) and protect the congregation over which they were appointed. They were never described as mediators of grace, nor is there any evidence in the New Testament of one person overseeing several congregations. In the earliest church, congregations are autonomous, meaning each congregation is overseen by its own plurality of elders.

---

4. Bailey, *Petrine Claims*, 45–48; McBrien, *Lives of the Popes*, xvi–xvii.

CONCLUSION

The Catholic doctrines of holy orders, the priesthood, and the papacy reflect a long-standing tradition. These teachings, however, diverge from the practices and theology of the first-century church. A biblical response suggests that while leadership and order are important in the life of the church, they should be grounded in the priesthood of all believers, the sufficiency of Christ's sacrifice, and the direct access every believer has to God through Christ alone. The New Testament presents a model of shared leadership among congregational elders, accountability to Scripture, and spiritual equality among believers, rather than a hierarchical and sacramental system centered on the papacy and a separate priesthood.

To be sure, many Protestant denominations do not hold to a biblical model of leadership either. A one-man pastorate is not biblical for the same reasons noted above. If a congregation is going to be scriptural, it *must* have a plurality of qualified men to serve as elders and deacons.

7

Marian Dogmas

THE VIRGIN MARY HOLDS a special place of veneration in the theology of Roman Catholicism. The Catholic Church has developed a series of dogmas about Mary that shape the faith and devotion of millions of its adherents. In fact, to reject any of these dogmas is to reject the Church and thus reject salvation. These dogmas—Mary's divine motherhood, her perpetual virginity, her Immaculate Conception, and her assumption into heaven—are considered infallible teachings that all Catholics must believe. Marian devotion including titles such as "Queen of Heaven" and practices such as praying the rosary are also deeply embedded in Catholic spirituality. While Catholic theology claims that Marian dogmas magnify Christ by honoring her as his mother, this chapter will analyze each dogma with reference to the CCC and then offer a response that questions the scriptural foundation of these teachings.

THE DIVINE MOTHERHOOD OF MARY

The Catholic Church teaches that Mary is the "Mother of God" (*Theotokos*), a title affirmed at the Council of Ephesus in AD 431 and reiterated in CCC 495.

> Called in the Gospels "the mother of Jesus," Mary is acclaimed by Elizabeth, at the prompting of the Spirit and even before the birth of her son, as "the mother of my Lord." In fact, the One whom she

conceived as man by the Holy Spirit . . . was none other than the Father's eternal Son, the second person of the Holy Trinity. Hence the Church confesses that Mary is truly "Mother of God" (*Theotokos*).

The title "Mother of God" reflects the reality that Jesus is both fully God and fully man. While Scripture affirms that Mary was the mother of Jesus (Luke 1:31), and that Jesus is divine (John 1:1, 14), the title of *Theotokos* can be misleading if it implies that Mary is the source of Christ's divinity. Biblically, Mary is the mother of Jesus's humanity, not his divine nature, which is eternal and uncreated (John 8:58). The New Testament never uses the title "Mother of God," and the earliest Christians focused their worship and devotion on Christ alone.

According to Catholic teaching, Mary remained a virgin before, during, and after the birth of Jesus.

> The deepening of faith in the virginal motherhood led the Church to confess Mary's real and perpetual virginity even in the act of giving birth to the Son of God made man (CCC 499).

The New Testament includes several references that challenge the idea of Mary's perpetual virginity. For instance, Matt 1:25 states that Joseph "did not know her *until* she had given birth to a son" (emphasis added), implying normal marital relations afterward. Mark 6:3 names Jesus's brothers and sisters, which in the normal usage of Greek (*adelphoi*) refers to biological siblings. The Roman Catholic Church teaches that *adelphoi* in this context refers to Jesus's cousins or close relatives, not biological siblings (CCC 500). However, this clearly changes the meaning of the words to mean something neither the context nor the word itself demands. Greek has a word for "cousin" (*anepsios*). If the people in question are not Jesus's literal brothers and sisters, why use the term when another one would have been perfectly acceptable?

THE IMMACULATE CONCEPTION

Most people think of the Immaculate Conception as the doctrine of Christ's birth without sin. However, the doctrine of the Immaculate Conception actually refers to the belief that Mary was preserved free from original sin from the moment of her conception. The doctrine was proclaimed by Pope Pius IX in 1854 and is summarized in CCC 491 and 492.

> Through the centuries the Church has become ever more aware that Mary, "full of grace" through God, was redeemed from the moment of her conception.
>
> The splendor of an entirely unique holiness by which Mary is "enriched from the first instant of her conception" comes wholly from Christ.

Of course, the Bible never teaches that Mary was without sin. The doctrine of the Immaculate Conception is absent from Scripture and was not formally declared until the nineteenth century. In fact, Rom 3:23 says, "All have sinned and fall short of the glory of God." Mary herself confesses her need for a Savior in Luke 1:47 when she says, "My spirit rejoices in *God my Savior*" (emphasis added). Additionally, the greeting "full of grace" in Luke 1:28 does not imply sinlessness but favor from God.

THE ASSUMPTION OF MARY

The Catholic Church teaches that Mary was assumed body and soul into heaven at the end of her earthly life. This was declared dogma by Pope Pius XII in 1950.

> The Immaculate Virgin, preserved free from all stain of original sin, when the course of her earthly life was finished, was taken up body and soul into heavenly glory (CCC 966).

The New Testament is silent on the end of Mary's earthly life, and no early Christian writings provide a definitive historical account. However, from the fourth century onward, apocryphal texts such as the *Transitus Mariae* ("Passing of Mary") circulated in both Eastern and Western Christianity describing Mary's peaceful death and bodily assumption into heaven. By the sixth century, liturgical feasts celebrating her "Dormition" (falling asleep) and "Assumption" had become common in the East, especially in Byzantine Christianity, and were gradually adopted in the West. The feast was celebrated in Rome by the seventh century. Church fathers such as John Damascene (d. ca. 750) defended the Assumption in homilies, arguing that it was fitting for the Mother of God not to see bodily corruption, given her sinless life and unique role in salvation history.[1]

---

1. See Pseudo-Melito, *Passing of the Virgin*, 475–85; John, *On the Dormition of Mary*, hom. 1–3.

MARIAN DEVOTION AND TITLES

Catholic spirituality includes many devotional practices directed toward Mary, including praying the rosary (which I will address in the next chapter), Marian feast days, pilgrimages, and prayers such as the "Hail Holy Queen." Titles attributed to Mary include "Queen of Heaven," "Mediatrix," and "Co-Redemptrix." The CCC notes, "The Church's devotion to the Blessed Virgin is intrinsic to Christian worship" (CCC 971). It also teaches that Mary "continues to bring us the gifts of eternal salvation" (CCC 969).

On the other hand, Protestants certainly go too far when they refuse any veneration of Mary. Her song proclaims, "From now on all generations will call me blessed" (Luke 1:48b), and should thus be respected as such. However, being blessed, respected, and venerated are not synonymous with or even worthy of worship. While Mary is honored in Scripture as the mother of Jesus and as a model of faith, she is never portrayed as an object of prayer or devotion. Christ alone is the mediator between God and humanity (1 Tim 2:5). Mary is not a partner with Christ in his redemptive scheme. She is not all knowing or ever present. The New Testament places Jesus as the sole redeemer (Heb 7:25). Nowhere in the New Testament are believers instructed to pray to Mary or seek her intercession. She is a wonderful example of motherhood and true femininity, but she is a person like all other people.

A LOGICAL ISSUE WITH MARIAN DOGMAS

At the heart of Marian dogma is the belief that Mary was born without sin and remained a virgin even in her marriage to Joseph. We have already noted issues with the idea of perpetual virginity from the text of Scripture; however, a larger issue arises from such a doctrine. The Catholic Church places an immense emphasis on marriage. Marriage is one of the seven sacraments of the church and is useful for the fulfilling of the command to "be fruitful and multiply" (Gen 1:28). The Catholic Church teaches that marriage is a sacred, lifelong covenant between a man and a woman, ordained by God for the mutual good of the spouses and the procreation and education of children. Thus, Catholic doctrine holds that the marital act must always remain open to the possibility of life. Consequently, Catholicism opposes artificial contraception, arguing that it deliberately frustrates the procreative purpose of sex and separates the unitive and procreative dimensions of marriage. The Catholic Church teaches that sex within marriage is a sacred and holy act intended to express the full, mutual self-giving of spouses in love and to remain open to the gift of life. The Catechism affirms that sexual intimacy is an expression of love and communion within the marriage. In 1 Cor 7:3–5, Paul emphasizes the mutual rights and responsibilities of spouses over each other's bodies by instructing them not to deprive one another except by mutual consent for a time of prayer. This passage affirms that sexual relations in marriage are good and necessary. It also highlights the equality of the spouses in the sexual dimension of marriage by reinforcing the belief that sexual union is both a duty and a gift rooted in love and self-sacrifice.

Therein lies the logical issue with Marian dogmas. If Mary remained a virgin, she would have been denying Joseph of his sexual needs and thereby did not fulfill her role as his wife. Additionally, Mary's perpetual virginity implies that she was not open to bringing in new life with her husband. On the other hand, if Mary did (as Scripture indicates) have other children, the doctrine of her perpetual virginity cannot stand. Either Mary was a perpetual virgin and did not keep with the Catholic teaching of marriage—which as a supposed sinless being, she must have done—or Mary was not a perpetual virgin. In either case, Mary cannot be held to the standard to which Catholicism raises her.

CONCLUSION

The four Marian dogmas—Divine Motherhood, perpetual virginity, Immaculate Conception, and Assumption—are central to Catholic theology as reinforced by the CCC. The New Testament presents Mary as a faithful servant of God and a remarkable woman, but not as sinless, perpetually virgin, or assumed bodily into heaven. In fact, Scripture states the opposite in some cases. Most significantly, the elevation of Mary as an object of veneration conflicts with the biblical focus on Christ as the sole source of salvation. A balanced biblical approach honors Mary's role without distorting the unique mediatory and redemptive work of Jesus Christ.

Postscript

I have discussed this doctrine with many Catholic friends. Each one assured me that the Catholic Church does not "worship" Mary. Wrestling with this idea, I had to define "worship" according to the standard of the New Testament. Worship is the act of giving praise, honor, and glory to an entity, whether deserving or not. Just as the pagans of the first century worshiped their idols, sometimes we too worship the idols of money, fame, power, sex, and pleasure. In the same vein, prayer to Mary, forming statues of her, and the belief that she is omniscient and omnipresent implies worship. Recently, a Catholic podcaster (who I respect greatly) put as a caption for a YouTube video, "Catholics worship Mary, and you should, too."[2] The issue here is not about admiring the mother of our Lord. It is about giving her praise and worship that should be and must be directed at the sovereign Godhead alone.

---

2. As I went back to look for the video, the podcaster in question had removed it. I do not want to speculate as to why. However, the material in the clip can be found in the full-length discussion at the 01:23 timestamp of Fradd, "7 Things Protestants Misunderstand."

8

The Rosary and Why I Own One

THE ROSARY IS A devotional prayer tool closely associated with Roman Catholicism. The rosary, though a relatively recent addition to Christian discipline throughout the course of church history, has evolved over many centuries. Before the formal rosary existed, early Christians employed repetitive prayers including the Lord's Prayer and some of the psalms to sanctify the hours of the day. For example, the Benedictine monks would pray the psalms regularly, but because many laypeople were illiterate and could not memorize or recite the entire Psalter, a simpler method arose that substituted 150 "Our Fathers" (i.e., the model prayer from Matt 6:5–15) for the 150 psalms.

In the twelfth century, the use of prayer beads became common in monastic and lay settings. The term *rosarium* (Latin for "rose garden") was first used in the context of prayer collections dedicated to the Virgin Mary. Thus, the rosary symbolizes a spiritual bouquet offered to Mary. By the thirteenth century, the practice of praying 150 "Hail Marys" (also called Ave Marias) divided into groups of fifty began to gain traction. Each group, called a "decade," included one "Our Father" and ten "Hail Marys." The grouping of prayers with meditations on the life of Christ and Mary created a meditative rhythm.

Traditionally, the Catholic Church credits St. Dominic (1170–221), founder of the Dominican Order, with receiving the rosary from the Virgin Mary during an apparition (i.e., a supposed appearance of Mary to

St. Dominic). According to this legend, Mary gave Dominic the rosary to combat the Albigensian heresy. This heresy asserted the coexistence of two mutually opposed principles—one good, the other evil. This doctrine stated that the former was the creator of the spiritual realm in which all is perfect and harmonious while the latter was the creator of the evil material world. The rosary then places the emphasis on the spiritual with prayer enacted by a physical device. While this story is widely accepted in Catholic devotional literature, historical evidence for the apparition is lacking. It is more likely that the Dominicans later popularized the rosary through their preaching and teaching.

By the fifteenth century, the structure of the rosary began to resemble what is practiced today. A Dominican friar, Alanus de Rupe (1428–75), is credited with formalizing the fifteen mysteries of the rosary and establishing confraternities to promote its recitation.[1] These so-called "mysteries" are grouped into three sets: the joyful, the sorrowful, and the glorious, each with five episodes from the lives of Jesus and Mary. This development solidified the rosary as both a prayer and a method of meditation.

Throughout history, many popes have promoted the rosary as a powerful spiritual weapon. Pope Pius V credited the rosary with the Christian victory over the Ottoman Empire at the Battle of Lepanto in 1571 and established October 7 as the feast of Our Lady of the Rosary. In 2002, Pope John Paul II added the Luminous Mysteries to the rosary, reflecting on significant moments in Jesus's public ministry. John Paul II's apostolic letter *Rosarium Virginis Mariae* reinvigorated Catholic appreciation for the rosary as a compilation of the gospel.

THE PRAYERS OF THE ROSARY

At its core, the rosary is a prayer tool. While the rosary can be blessed, not all rosaries carry papal or priestly blessings. Even so, rosaries are also believed to ward off demons and other evil spirits. However, the rosary is primarily used for spiritual meditation in the course of prayer. The five prayers of the rosary center on devotion to the Catholic Church and Marian dogmas. We will address these issues below.

---

1. Thurston, "Confraternity," 227.

Section One

Prayer 1: The Sign of the Cross and Apostles' Creed

The rosary begins with the sign of the cross (i.e., making the shape of the cross by touching one's head, chest, left shoulder, and right shoulder, although the Eastern Orthodox reverse the shoulder directions) and the Apostles' Creed. This creed is a concise summary of Christian belief and sets the tone for the spiritual focus of the coming prayers. It acknowledges core doctrines such as the Trinity, the incarnation, and the resurrection.

The Apostles' Creed

I believe in God the Father Almighty, Maker of heaven and earth,
And in Jesus Christ, his only Son our Lord,
Who was conceived by the Holy Spirit,
Born of the Virgin Mary,
Suffered under Pontius Pilate,
Was crucified, dead, and buried.
He descended into hell;[2]
The third day he rose again from the dead;
He ascended into heaven,
And sitteth on the right hand of God the Father Almighty;
From thence he shall come to judge the quick and the dead.
I believe in the Holy Spirit;
The Holy catholic Church, the Communion of Saints;
The Forgiveness of sins;
The Resurrection of the body,
And the Life everlasting.
Amen.

---

2. The reference to Christ's descent into hell comes from 1 Pet 3:18–22 and Eph 4:9. First Peter 3:19 states that after Christ's death he went and preached to the spirits in prison. Commentators see this event as (1) Christ's announcement of his victory over evil to fallen angels who led the Noahic generation into sin or (2) Christ's preaching of repentance through Noah to the unrighteous humans who are now dead but lived in the days of Noah. The traditional view understands it as a reference to the underworld (i.e., hell), where Jesus is thought to have descended in the three days between his death and resurrection. A second option is to translate the phrase "of the earth" as a genitive of apposition: "to the lower parts, namely, the earth." Some scholars hold this view, arguing that it refers to the incarnation. A third option, which also sees the phrase "of the earth" as a genitive of apposition, is that the descent refers to the descent of the Spirit at Pentecost (cf. Acts 4:11–16). Support for this latter view is found in the intertestamental use of Ps 68:18 (quoted in v. 8), which is consistently interpreted as a reference to Moses's ascent of Mt. Sinai to "capture" the words of the law.

Prayer 2: The Our Father (*Pater Noster*)

Each decade of the rosary begins with the "Lord's Prayer," or better called "the Model Prayer." Jesus, in Luke 11:2–4, presents this prayer after his disciples ask him how they ought to pray and is mentioned in Matt 6:9–13 in his Sermon on the Mount. The prayer centers on the holiness of God, submission to his will, dependence on his provision, his forgiveness, and his protection, namely from evil. The use of the Our Father in the rosary echoes early monastic traditions.

The Our Father

Our Father who art in heaven, hallowed be thy name.
Thy kingdom come, thy will be done on earth as it is in heaven.
Give us this day our daily bread.
And forgive us our trespasses,
as we forgive those who trespass against us.
And lead us not into temptation, but deliver us from evil.
Amen.

Prayer 3: The Hail Mary (*Ave Maria*)

The Hail Mary is the most repeated prayer in the rosary. It is based on two greetings to Mary in Scripture: (1) Gabriel's words in Luke 1:28, "Hail, full of grace, the Lord is with thee," and (2) Elizabeth's words in Luke 1:42, "Blessed are you among women, and blessed is the fruit of your womb." The second half of the prayer—"Holy Mary, Mother of God, pray for us sinners now and at the hour of our death"—is a later, nonbiblical addition requesting Mary's intercession.

The Hail Mary

Hail Mary, full of grace, the Lord is with thee.
Blessed art thou among women,
and blessed is the fruit of thy womb, Jesus.
Holy Mary, Mother of God, pray for us sinners,
now and at the hour of our death.
Amen.

Prayer 4: The Glory Be (Doxology)

After each decade, the "Glory Be" is recited. This doxology, while not a direct quotation of Scripture, reflects the Trinitarian praise found throughout the Bible (e.g., Jude 25; Rev 5:13). It offers a moment to transition from one mystery to the next while reinforcing a Christ-centered theology.

The Glory Be

Glory be to the Father,
and to the Son,
and to the Holy Spirit,
as it was in the beginning,
is now, and ever shall be,
world without end.
Amen.

Prayer 5: The Mysteries of the Rosary

The rosary's meditative core involves contemplating specific events called "mysteries" within salvation history. There are four mysteries, the fourth of which was added by Pope John Paul II in October of 2002. They are: (1) *Joyful Mysteries*, which are the Annunciation, Visitation, Nativity, Presentation, Finding in the Temple (recited on Monday and Saturday); (2) *Sorrowful Mysteries*, which are the Agony in the Garden, Scourging, Crowning with Thorns, Carrying the Cross, Crucifixion (recited on Tuesday and Friday); (3) *Glorious Mysteries*, which are the Resurrection, Ascension, Pentecost, Assumption of Mary, Coronation of Mary (recited on Wednesday and Sunday); (4) *Luminous Mysteries* (added in 2002), which are the Baptism of Jesus, Wedding at Cana, Proclamation of the Kingdom, Transfiguration, Institution of the Eucharist (recited on Thursday). These mysteries are meditated upon after saying various other prayers according to their order.

VAIN REPETITION?

One of the primary criticisms of the rosary is that it employs "vain repetitions," which are condemned by Jesus in Matt 6:7. Is that a fair critique? Below is an excerpt from my master's thesis on the spiritual disciplines.

This will frame our response to the use of the rosary and the condemnation of vain repetitions in prayer. The following passages from Matt 6:5–15 are the author's translation.

Matthew 6:5–6

> And when you are praying, do not be as the hypocrites; for they love, [both] in the synagogues and on the corners of the streets, to stand and to pray, so that they may be seen by others; truly I say to you, they have received their reward. But when you pray, go into your storeroom and close your door and pray to your Father, the one who is in secret; and your Father, the one seeing in secret, will reward you.

Prayer engages us with God.[3] Prayer was a fundamental part of Jewish piety. The Jews had adopted a posture of prayer where they would stand with their hands and head lifted towards heaven (cf. Luke 18:11). This is different from the traditional posture of prayer in our modern day where heads are often bowed and hands are clasped together.

Verse 5 presents both religious and nonreligious settings. The Jews had developed three periods of the day in which they would turn towards the temple and pray (cf. Dan 6:13). These times were 9:00 a.m., 12:00 p.m., and 3:00 p.m. 9:00 a.m. and 3:00 p.m. also marked times of sacrifice at the temple. Thus, the Jewish leaders often planned to be in public places when the time came to offer their prayers.

The "wide streets" differ from the "narrow streets" presented in Matt 6:2. The narrow streets were for traveling purposes, while the wide streets referred to marketplaces comparable to town squares.[4] Both places (i.e., the synagogues and the street corners) were public. The antithesis is presented in v. 6. Jesus suggests prayer should take place within the innermost secret room where only the one praying and God are present. Jesus often secluded himself to pray in the most trying of times (e.g., Matt 26:36–46). As with Matt 6:3, Jesus is not suggesting the only acceptable way to pray is by locking oneself in a closet. Jesus is exaggerating to highlight the necessity of one's private, internal righteousness.

---

3. Nolland, *Matthew*, 277.
4. Rogers and Rogers, *Key to the Greek New Testament*, 13.

The hypocrites stand in the synagogues and street corners to be "seen by people." This echoes v. 2 where the hypocrites give only to be seen by others. However, there is a deeper meaning to the word *phainomia* here. This term means "to appear" or "to show oneself." This presents a completely different connotation than the traditional term *blepō*, which is the verb used of God. The hypocrites desire to be noticed, while God is the one who sees both in public and private.

Matthew 6:7–15

> But when you pray, do not babble as the gentiles, for they think they will be heard and answered because of their many words. Do not be like them, for your Father knows the needs you all have before you all ask him. Therefore, you pray like this; "Our Father, the one who is in heaven, holy is your name; let your kingdom come, let your will come to pass just as in heaven also on earth. Give to us this day our bread today; and cancel out our debts, as we also canceled out the ones indebted to us; and do not lead us into a trial; but rescue us from the evil one." For if we forgive the failures of others, so also your heavenly Father will forgive you; but if you do not forgive others, neither will your heavenly Father forgive your failures.

It is important to understand that this prayer is a model from which our own prayers are to be designed. Jesus begins the model prayer with a rebuke of gentilic prayer methods. These pagan worshipers were well known for prayers that consisted of "many words" (*battalogeō*), a hopoxlogomina in the New Testament. These "many words" could refer to the pagan chants used in magical formulas and rituals. However, Garland argues this babbling refers to various aliases of the gods.[5] The gentiles would call out these names in great length and detail in hopes that the gods would show them favor for their dedication.[6] Nolland argues the meaning is derived from the Greek root *bat(t)*, meaning "stuttering."[7]

God does not give his attention based on who can flatter him the most. God knows that he is the only true and living God (cf. Isa 44:9–20). God does not give humanity his ear because humanity begs. He listens to

---

5. Rogers and Rogers, *Key to the Greek New Testament*, 13.
6. Garland, "Lord's Prayer," 216.
7. Nolland, *Matthew*, 284.

the needs of his creation because he loves and cares for his creation. Jesus states that the Father knows what one needs before one asks (Matt 6:8).

Jesus then gives his model for prayer. Jesus gives a title, proof of essence, and a description of God in v. 9. The title is "Father." This term does not represent familial linage but a relationship between God and his children (cf. Eph 1:5; 1 John 3:1). The proof of his essence is described as "the one who is in heaven." This phrase describes God's spiritual nature. Too often prayers are offered whimsically. The standard "Dear Heavenly Father" introduction begins half-heartedly and the remainder of the prayer seems to only be about one's physical desires. God is holy. As his throne is approached, the one offering the prayer must remember God's character.

Through the course of this section, I have mostly agreed with John Nolland's syntax and exegesis. Verse 10, however, is where I must offer a different analysis. Nolland argues v. 10 is "clearly eschatologically oriented."[8] Perhaps the Jews would have interpreted the kingdom language in this way; however, a further reading of the New Testament, namely the Epistles, will prove the kingdom's identity and purpose. The Gospels present the kingdom as a future occurrence (cf. Matt 3:2; 4:17; 6:10; 16:19; Mark 1:15). In the Epistles, the kingdom is present and active (cf. Rom 14:17; 1 Cor 6:9; Acts 28:31). As Paul says in Rom 14:17, "For the kingdom of God is not a matter of eating and drinking but of righteousness and peace and joy in the Holy Spirit."

Though Jesus commands prayer for the coming of the kingdom, this does not mean that Christians should not pray for the kingdom that is now here. Additionally, Christians should pray for the coming of the King (cf. Jude 20–21). Furthermore, Christians should pray about things concerning the kingdom, such as its expansion and prosperity. This is accomplished by praying for the will of God to be done on earth as it is in heaven. The Greek term *thelēma* ("will") is also used in conjunction with obedience in Matt 7:21, 12:50, and 18:14. Paul discusses the will of God further in Rom 12:2: "And do not be conformed to this world, but be transformed by the renewing of your mind, so that you may prove what the will of God is, that which is good and acceptable and perfect."

Verse 11 presents the only petition for physical necessity in the model prayer. The petition is made for God to give enough physical sustenance to last for one day. This does not suggest that Christians cannot pray for other physical needs. James 5:13–20 notes that Christians can and should pray

---

8. Nolland, *Matthew*, 287.

for the sick and suffering. Even so, spiritual matters should consume our prayers rather than petitions for physical wants of the world.

The need to be forgiven is coupled with the need to offer forgiveness. Matthew 6:14–15 connects the forgiving of one another with being forgiven by God. Pettigrove adds, "In the New Testament, forgiving is principally something one does and only derivatively something one feels."[9] Forgiveness is an action. Nolland explains, "It is to say that failure to forgive closes the door to ongoing forgiveness (cf. Matt 18:23–35)." Matthew uses legal terms for sin and forgiveness that describe a debt that must be paid in full. Forgiveness then is the cancelation of these debts. Matthew as a tax collector would have been familiar with the legal cancelation of debts and the importance of having a debt no longer owed.

Verse 13 seems to contradict the nature of God presented in Jas 1:13. God cannot be tempted and does not tempt anyone. However, the Model Prayer makes a petition for God not to lead his followers into temptation. The OT shows God being quite comfortable with testing various subjects. The LXX uses the term *peirasmos*, which is generally more in line with an experience coming directly from the hand of God.[10] The petition mentioned in the Model Prayer is simply for God to lead his followers into positive situations rather than those of evil.

The NASB, ESV, and KJV say, "Deliver us from evil." The LITV and YLT read "deliver us from *the* evil" (emphasis added). The ASV uses the definite article and adds "one" in italicized font after "evil." Is the plea for one to be rescued from *evil* as some abstract idea to which all of humanity falls or from *the evil one*?

Nolland notes that *ponēros* (evil) refers simply to that which harms.[11] It is a word that does not necessarily encompass wickedness but places the emphasis on the one committing the act. Therefore, Nolland explains, a natural disaster can be as evil as murder. Nolland translates the phrase, "Rescue us, instead, from [that which is] evil." My translation differs: "but rescue us from the evil one." Both translations emphasize the ablative of separation emphasized by the preposition *apo*. I have interpreted the definite article as an identifier of *evil* while Nolland interprets it as a relative pronoun.

---

9. Pettigrove, "Forgiveness and Interpretation," 430.
10. Nolland, *Matthew*, 291–92. Also note Job 2:10.
11. Nolland, *Matthew*, 293.

It is necessary to stop here and briefly address the textual variant presented in v. 13. The evidence overwhelmingly suggests the omission of the phrase, "For yours is the kingdom and the power and the glory forever. Amen." However, Jewish prayer was often concluded by a doxology; for a Jew to do otherwise was unthinkable.[12] However, Codex Sinaiticus (fourth century) and Codex Vaticanus (fourth century) both omit this phrase along with other significant uncial manuscripts.[13] Further, Origen (253), Cyril of Jerusalem (386), and Gregory of Nyssa (394) show no knowledge of this phrase. Jerome adds "amen" to the end of the prayer but nothing else. However, Codex Regius (eighth century), Sangallensis (ninth century), and Koridethi (ninth century) all include this phrase as well as a multitude of miniscule manuscripts. However, these manuscripts are later witnesses. The phrase is most likely not original to the text and may have been inserted due to a harmonization with 1 Chr 29:11–13. There is no reason to believe a scribe would have omitted the phrase. The editors of the UBS Greek New Testament fifth addition argue for the omission of the doxology with an "A" rating, meaning they feel overwhelmingly confident that the doxology is not original.

VAIN REPETITIONS AND THE OUR FATHER

In the previous section, we noted that the phrase "vain repetitions" in its Greco-Roman context does not refer to repeating a prayer over and over but to an attempt to gain the attention of the gods with flattery. In this case, the evangelical argument that the rosary offers "vain repetitions" is invalid. Protestants need not use this argument, especially when Protestant worship music repeats its chorus five thousand times before the song ends.

The above exegesis has explored in detail the Greek formulation of each verse. In this sense, one may wonder how anyone could promote the recitation of this prayer for two primary reasons. First, the prayer is a model, not a script. Our prayers should include acknowledgement of God, prayer for the kingdom, prayer for physical issues, and prayer for forgiveness. Jesus's words to "pray in this way" are not synonymous with "pray this exact prayer." Second, some aspects of the prayer do not apply now in the way they did then—namely in the prayer for the coming of the kingdom.

---

12. Luz, *Matthew 1—7*, 385.
13. See Codices D; Z; 0170.

Thus, if we pray the rosary and thereby pray the Our Father, we are praying for things that have already come.

Although we did not cover the Hail Mary specifically earlier, we must address it now. While it includes phrases taken directly from Scripture (Luke 1:28; Luke 1:42), these are greetings directed to Mary by the angel Gabriel and her cousin Elizabeth, not prayers. In Scripture, there is no indication that believers are to use these greetings as a form of prayer, nor are believers ever instructed to address Mary in prayer at all. The Bible reserves prayer for communication with God alone (Phil 4:6; Matt 6:9).

Moreover, the second half of the Hail Mary—"Holy Mary, Mother of God, pray for us sinners now and at the hour of our death"—has absolutely no biblical foundation. Nowhere in the Bible are Christians instructed to seek intercession from the dead, including Mary. On the contrary, 1 Tim 2:5 clearly teaches that "there is one God, and there is one mediator between God and men, the man Christ Jesus." This exclusive role of Christ as mediator means that prayer should be directed through him alone. Invoking Mary as an intercessor elevates her role in a way that is not supported by the teachings or practices of the early church as recorded in the New Testament.

Finally, the Hail Mary reflects a theology of Marian veneration that exceeds what the Bible permits. As we noted in the last chapter, although Mary is honored as the mother of Jesus and is called "blessed among women," she is not given a role of spiritual authority in Scripture. For example, when a woman in the crowd called out, "Blessed is the womb that bore you," Jesus replied, "Blessed rather are those who hear the word of God and keep it" (Luke 11:27–28). Even Jesus shifted the focus from Mary's maternity to the obedience of discipleship. The Hail Mary encourages a focus on Mary that diverts attention from Christ who is the true object of prayer and devotion.

The New Testament provides ample teaching on how believers are to pray "in the Spirit" (Eph 6:18), "without ceasing" (1 Thess 5:17), with thanksgiving (Phil 4:6), and in Jesus's name (John 14:13–14). These prayers are relational, Spirit-led, and directed to the Father through Christ. No system of beads, mysteries, or ritual formulae is necessary for true communion with God.

WHY I OWN A ROSARY

If the rosary includes prayers and creeds that are not biblical, why do I own one? The answer is simple. I do not pray the rosary per se. When my daughter was born, I was spending a lot of time tending to her and her mother; however, I noticed that I was not spending as much time in Bible reading and prayer as I had previously done. When I would pray, I would get distracted to the point of not finishing the prayer. So, I bought a rosary. My rosary does not have an image of Christ on the crucifix, but other than that, it is a traditional rosary. I use the beads to mark individuals and problems for which I should pray. Each bead helps me remember to pray for someone or something specific. I find using the rosary no different than using a prayer app or making a prayer list.

CONCLUSION

The rosary developed over centuries to promote meditation on the life of Christ and devotion to Mary. Its prayers form a rhythm of contemplative repetition. However, from a biblical standpoint, the practice lacks apostolic precedent, elevates Mary's role to an intercessor of prayer, and diverts attention from Christ in salvation history. For Christians seeking fidelity to the New Testament pattern, prayer should remain God-centered, Scripture-guided, and Christ-mediated. The issue is not with the tool itself but with the meaning ascribed to the tool.

9

The Canonization of Saints

THE DOCTRINE OF SAINTHOOD in the Catholic Church teaches that the saints actively intercede for the faithful by having direct access to God in heaven. However, for many non-Catholics, particularly those from Protestant traditions, the Catholic doctrine of saints raises concerns. According to the CCC, saints are individuals who have lived lives of "heroic virtue" and now reside in heaven in the beatific vision (CCC 1023). Catholicism teaches that these individuals, whether officially canonized or not, constitute the "Church triumphant" and are in communion with the Catholic Church on earth and in purgatory (CCC 954). The term "saint" originates from the Latin *sanctus*, meaning "holy."

The communion of saints is a central concept in Catholic ecclesiology. It signifies the spiritual solidarity among the faithful on earth (Church militant), the souls undergoing purification (Church suffering), and the blessed in heaven (Church triumphant) (CCC 946–62). This communion is rooted in the unity of the body of Christ, and through it, spiritual goods are shared among all members (CCC 949).

The CCC teaches that saints intercede for the living, and that their prayers are effective because they are united more perfectly to Christ (CCC 956). This belief is often supported by references to Jas 5:16, which states, "The prayer of a righteous person has great power as it is working." Catholicism teaches that this intercession is similar to earthly Christians praying for one another.

The Canonization of Saints

Saints only become so through a process called canonization—the formal process by which the Catholic Church declares sainthood on a deceased person. Canonization includes rigorous investigation into the person's life and the verification of miracles attributed to the individual. Once canonized, the individual is included in the liturgical calendar and may be publicly honored. The Catholic Church distinguishes between *latria* (worship due to God alone) and *dulia* (veneration given to saints), with *hyperdulia* reserved for the Virgin Mary (CCC 2132), though these designations often overlap in practice. For example, the saints are integrally woven into Catholic liturgical life. Their feast days, relics, and invocations feature prominently in Mass and the Liturgy of the Hours. The eucharistic prayers often include invocations of saints, notably Mary, Joseph, and the apostles.

The canonization of saints finds its rooting in some church fathers such as Augustine and Jerome who supported the practice of invoking saints. Augustine wrote, "We do not build temples to our martyrs as to gods, but memories of them as of men of God who have struggled for the truth, to the end that by remembering them we may imitate their faith" (*Answer to Faustus* 20.21). These traditions maintained through councils and magisterial teachings contribute to the doctrinal formulation of the communion and veneration of saints.

THE PROCESS OF CANONIZATION

The canonization of saints in Roman Catholicism is a detailed and multi-step process by which the deceased individual is formally declared as having lived a life of heroic virtue and thus is now in heaven and able to intercede on behalf of the faithful. The process of canonization is rooted in centuries of tradition but has developed into a formal juridical procedure codified by the Catholic Church and overseen by the Dicastery for the Causes of Saints.

The process begins at the diocesan level and follows four primary stages: Servant of God, Venerable, Blessed, and finally, Saint. Before any formal proceedings begin, there must be at least five years since the candidate's death, although the pope can waive this waiting period, as it was in the cases of Mother Teresa and Pope John Paul II (CCC 828). The bishop of the diocese in which the person died opens an initial investigation into the life, virtues, writings, and reputation for holiness or martyrdom of the individual. If sufficient evidence exists, the bishop sends the findings to the

Vatican's Dicastery for the Causes of Saints. At this point, the individual is given the title "Servant of God."

The Vatican's dicastery appoints a postulator to gather further documentation and prepare a formal report called a *positio*, which is evaluated by a group of theologians. If the theologians and the cardinals of the dicastery agree that the person exhibited heroic virtue or was martyred for the faith, the pope may then declare the person "Venerable" (cf. Congregation for the Causes of Saints, *Sanctorum Mater*, 2007).

For the next stage—beatification—one miracle attributed to the intercession of the candidate after their death is required, except in the case of martyrs. This miracle must be rigorously investigated and authenticated. If the miracle is approved, the pope may declare the person "Blessed." This allows for limited public veneration, typically within the local diocese, region, or religious community (CCC 828).

The final step—canonization—requires a second verified miracle following beatification. This, too, is not required for martyrs. Once this second miracle is approved, the pope can declare the person a "Saint," allowing universal veneration in the liturgy of the Catholic Church. The formal canonization ceremony is a solemn papal act and includes a Mass of canonization during which the pope reads the decree and inserts the saint's name into the canon, or official list, of recognized saints.

Canonization does not "make" a person a saint per se but publicly confirms what is already believed to be true—that the person is in heaven and worthy of universal veneration and imitation. As the CCC states, "By canonizing some of the faithful . . . the Church recognizes the power of the Spirit of holiness . . . and sustains the hope of believers by proposing the saints to them as models and intercessors" (CCC 828).

A BIBLICAL EVALUATION OF THE DOCTRINE OF SAINTS

The Catholic teaching that the saints in heaven intercede for the faithful on earth is grounded in the Catholic understanding of the "Communion of Saints," a doctrine codified in the CCC.

> Being more closely united to Christ, those who dwell in heaven fix the whole Church more firmly in holiness. . . . They do not cease to intercede with the Father for us (CCC 956).

Their intercession is their most exalted service to God's plan. (CCC 2683).

Catholic theologians cite Rev 5:8 as a scriptural image of this heavenly intercession. According to this view, the "golden bowls full of incense" symbolize the saints' prayers. Notably, the Douay-Rheims Bible, the Catholic English translation from the Latin Vulgate, renders the passage "golden vials full of odors, which are the prayers of saints."

Catholic exegesis identifies the "elders" as a class of glorified human beings (possibly patriarchs or saints) who are actively involved in worship and intercession. This notion is strengthened by cross-references such as Rev 8:3–4 where an angel presents incense "with the prayers of all the saints" before God's throne. Catholic scholars, such as Scott Hahn, argue that this scene reflects the liturgy of heaven and mirrors the earthly Mass where the faithful join with saints and angels in prayer.[1] The Catholic position is strengthened by seeing the heavenly liturgy in Revelation as prescriptive for earthly practice.

Regarding Rev 5:8, Protestant interpreters view the "prayers of the saints" as prayers offered by believers on earth, not *to* the saints, but *by* the saints to God. Thus, the elders are symbolic figures, not literal departed saints interceding for others. In this interpretation, the bowls represent the collected prayers of Christians presented to God as part of the heavenly worship scene. The incense here reflects Ps 141:2 where prayers are likened to incense also. J. Ramsey Michaels addresses the issue.

> Because there were elders in Israel and because many early Christian congregations were ruled by "elders" (Greek *presbyteroi*; Acts 14:23; 1 Tim 5:17; Jas 5:14; 1 Pet 5:1), it is commonly assumed that the *twenty-four elders* in some way represent the people of God (with twenty-four often explained as the sum of the twelve tribes of Israel and the twelve apostles). But there is no reason to assume that the elders represent anyone but themselves. In John's vision, they are simply heavenly beings of some sort, and it is best to leave it at that.[2]

Protestant critics argue that the Catholic use of Rev 5:8 goes beyond what the text actually says. The passage does not describe anyone praying to the elders or asking them for intercession. Rather, it shows elders in heaven

---

1. Hahn, *Lamb's Supper*, 130–40.
2. Michaels, *Revelation*, 92.

holding the prayers of the saints. Their identity is ambiguous. This interpretation suggests that Rev 5:8 illustrates how God values and receives the prayers of his people, but does not endorse praying to anyone other than to himself. The key distinction is between the content of the prayers (which come from believers) and the means of their presentation (symbolically offered in bowls of incense) without implying the necessity or propriety of invoking saints in prayer.

Many Catholics reference the Shepherd of Hermas (written ca. AD 90–150) as one of the earliest attestations of the intercession of saints. However, the Shepherd does not explicitly teach the intercession of the saints in the later Catholic sense—that is, invoking the departed righteous to pray on behalf of the living. However, some passages imply a communal concern between the righteous and the living, which later writers interpreted as an early form of intercession. One of the most relevant sections is where Hermas sees righteous people (symbolized by stones) being gathered into a tower and prays for the weak. The angel explains that the righteous already at rest are concerned for those still on earth, suggesting a kind of spiritual solidarity across the living and dead.

> These are those who have already fallen asleep, and they believed, and their spirits went out of their bodies . . . because they had walked in the uprightness of truth and kept the commandments of the Lord, they have a place with the righteous (Herm. Vis. 2.4.2).

Although the passage shows that the departed righteous are acknowledged and honored, it does not show them actively interceding for the living. Rather, it is Hermas himself who prays or intercedes. J. N. D. Kelly notes, "The practice of invoking the saints . . . can scarcely be traced earlier than the latter part of the third century. The Shepherd of Hermas speaks of the prayer of a righteous man being of great avail, but does not suggest that the departed saints intercede."[3]

Ultimately, the divergence hinges on differing understandings of mediation, intercession, and ecclesiology. The Catholic position incorporates both Scripture and the Tradition of the Church to defend its position, while the Protestant critique remains rooted in the principle of *sola scriptura*, emphasizing that Christ alone is sufficient for our access to God.

In the New Testament, the Greek term "saint" (*hagios*) is consistently applied to all believers, not a select group of canonized individuals. For

---

3. Kelly, *Early Christian Doctrines*, 490.

The Canonization of Saints

example, Paul addresses the churches in Rome, Corinth, and Ephesus as saints (Rom 1:7; 1 Cor 1:2; Eph 1:1). This usage indicates that sainthood is not a posthumous title for the especially virtuous but a designation for all those who have been sanctified in Christ.

Scripture emphatically declares that Jesus Christ is the sole mediator between God and man (1 Tim 2:5). The doctrine of the saintly intercession conflicts with this truth. While Catholic apologists argue that the saints participate in Christ's mediation, the New Testament offers no precedent for seeking intercession from the dead. In fact, the dead seem to have no interaction with the living (cf. 1 Cor 15:29).

The account of the rich man and Lazarus (Luke 16:19–31) provides compelling evidence that the dead cannot communicate with the living and thus cannot receive our prayers or act on our behalf. In the story, the rich man, tormented in Hades, pleads with Abraham to send Lazarus to warn his five brothers. Abraham firmly denies the request, stating that the living have Moses and the prophets, and if they do not listen to them, they will not be persuaded even if someone rises from the dead. Additionally, Lazarus is in a state of bliss and seems to have no access or desire to access the prayers of the living. This clear boundary between the living and the dead underscores the finality of death and the impossibility of interaction across that divide.

There is no example in the New Testament of believers praying to deceased saints. All recorded prayers are addressed to God the Father through Jesus Christ. The practice of invoking saints lacks direct scriptural endorsement and resembles the forbidden necromantic practices condemned in Deut 18:10–12: "There shall not be found among you anyone who burns his son or his daughter as an offering, anyone who practices divination or tells fortunes or interprets omens, or a sorcerer or a charmer or a medium or a necromancer or one who inquires of the dead, for whoever does these things is an abomination to the LORD. And because of these abominations the LORD your God is driving them out before you." The belief that saints can hear and respond to prayers from countless individuals worldwide implies omnipresence and omniscience—attributes reserved for God alone (Isa 42:8; Ps 139:1–12). The Bible does not suggest that glorified humans are granted such divine capacities.

CONCLUSION

Although the Catholic Church differentiates between worship and veneration, the line often becomes blurred in practice. Statues, candles, prayers, and feast days devoted to saints mimic acts of worship. Scripture sternly warns against idolatry (1 John 5:21). The New Testament promotes direct access to God through Christ (Heb 4:16). The "cloud of witnesses" in Heb 12:1 is meant as motivational imagery, not an invitation to invoke the dead. Paul repeatedly emphasizes the sufficiency of Christ for all spiritual needs (Col 2:9–10).

The doctrine of saints, as articulated by the Catholic Church, offers a theology that promotes imitation of virtue and spiritual intercession. However, when this doctrine is held against the standard of Scripture, several critical issues emerge. The preeminent issue is that the New Testament defines all those in Christ as saints while they are still alive. Additionally, Scripture restricts intercessory roles in prayer to the living and elevates Christ alone as the exclusive mediator of prayer to the Father. Furthermore, the lack of scriptural support for praying to saints, coupled with theological implications that verge on idolatry, underscores the need for caution. While remembering the faithful departed and learning from their examples is commendable, worship and spiritual dependence must remain directed to God through Christ alone.

10

Purgatory

THE DOCTRINE OF PURGATORY stands as one of the most distinctive teachings of the Roman Catholic Church. Though it shares affinities with broader Christian understandings of sanctification and judgment, the doctrine of purgatory posits an intermediate state after death in which souls destined for heaven undergo purification or the purging of their sins. This teaching has generated centuries of theological debate particularly between Catholics and Protestants. This chapter aims to present the Catholic doctrine of purgatory by tracing its development through the church fathers and the CCC and to provide a biblical response that challenges the necessity and coherence of the doctrine from a non-Catholic Christian perspective.

THE CATHOLIC DOCTRINE OF PURGATORY

The CCC defines purgatory as a place or condition of temporal punishment for those who, having died in God's grace and friendship, are still imperfectly purified.

> All who die in God's grace and friendship, but still imperfectly purified, are indeed assured of their eternal salvation; but after death they undergo purification, so as to achieve the holiness necessary to enter the joy of heaven (CCC 1030).

This concept hinges on two crucial Catholic beliefs: (1) the holiness of God requires complete purity from sin, and (2) the grace of God allows for a postmortem purification of the soul. The doctrine is distinct from hell (a place of eternal separation from God) and heaven (eternal union with God). Purgatory is thus a temporary state for the saved, though not purified from all sin.

THEOLOGICAL FOUNDATIONS FOR PURGATORY IN CATHOLIC THOUGHT

Catholic theologians point to several passages to support the idea of purgatory. Chief among them is 2 Macc 12:45, where Judas Maccabeus offers prayers for the dead by stating, "Therefore he made atonement for the dead, that they might be delivered from their sin." Although this book is considered apocryphal in Protestant traditions, it holds deuterocanonical status in the Catholic Church.[1] Other passages used to support purgatory include 1 Cor 3:13–15, "Each one's work will become manifest, for the Day will disclose it. . . . If any man's work is burned up, he will suffer loss, though he himself will be saved, but only as through fire," and Matt 12:32, "And whoever speaks a word against the Son of Man will be forgiven, but whoever speaks against the Holy Spirit will not be forgiven, either in this age or in the age to come." These verses are interpreted by Catholic theologians as implying a postmortem process whereby the soul is purified by divine fire.

THE DEVELOPMENT OF PURGATORY IN CHURCH HISTORY

Tertullian (ca. 160–225), while not yet articulating a fully developed doctrine of purgatory, spoke of prayers for the dead. He noted, "We offer sacrifices for the dead on their birthday anniversaries" (*The Crown* 3). Origen (ca. 184–253) developed the idea of a purifying fire when he wrote, "If a man departs this life with lighter faults, he is condemned to fire which burns away the lighter materials, preparing the soul for the kingdom of God" (*Homilies on Jeremiah* 20:3). Augustine of Hippo (354–430) believed in a purifying process after death. He wrote, "Temporal punishments are suffered by some in this life only, by some after death, by some both now

---

1. The term "deuterocanonical" refers to those books which are included in the Catholic Bible and are treated as uninspired but profitable for spiritual formation and learning.

and then; but all of them before that last and strictest judgment" (*The City of God* 21.13).

THOMAS AQUINAS ON PURGATORY

Thomas Aquinas in the *Summa Theologiae* articulated the nature of purgatorial suffering as being caused by a purifying fire distinct from the eternal torments of hell. Aquinas stressed that the souls in purgatory rejoice because their salvation is assured even as they endure cleansing pain. Aquinas affirms the existence of purgatory as a necessary part of divine justice when he writes, "It is sufficiently clear from what has been said that there is a Purgatory after this life. For those who depart from this life with venial sins, or without having satisfied for the punishment due to their sins, must be cleansed after death."[2] Here, he reasons that not all sins deserve eternal punishment, yet God's justice requires full satisfaction—hence, a temporal purging must exist.

Aquinas further asked if the punishment of Purgatory surpasses all temporal punishments of this life? Aquinas answers yes. The punishment of purgatory is greater than any suffering in earthly life. He writes, "The least pain of Purgatory surpasses the greatest pain of this life."[3] This is due to the purity of divine justice and the direct experience of loss of the beatific vision during the purging process.

Aquinas asserts that purgatory involves both (1) pain of loss (i.e., the delay in seeing God since the soul desires union with him) and (2) pain of sense (i.e., a literal suffering often interpreted metaphorically as fire). Aquinas says the fire of purgatory is the same as the fire of hell, but differs in its purpose. For Aquinas, fire purifies in purgatory and punishes eternally in hell.

Aquinas affirms that masses, prayers, and almsgiving by the living can reduce the time souls spend in purgatory. He writes, "Suffrages for the dead profit those who are in Purgatory as regards the remission of punishment."[4] He emphasizes the interconnectedness of the Church Militant and the Church Suffering. Though Aquinas acknowledges the pain of purgatory, he insists the souls in purgatory have assurance of salvation: "They are

---

2. Aquinas, *Summa Theologiae* Suppl., Q12, A1.
3. Aquinas, *Summa Theologiae* Suppl., app. 1, Q2, A1.
4. Aquinas, *Summa Theologiae* Suppl., Q71, A6.

in a state of grace and friendship with God, and their ultimate reward is certain."[5] This distinguishes purgatory from hell, where there is no hope.

SACRAMENTS AND INDULGENCES

As seen above with the teachings of Thomas Aquinas, the Catholic Church teaches that the living can assist the dead who are currently in purgatory through prayers, Masses, and indulgences. An indulgence is the remission of temporal punishment due to sin, granted by the Church under certain conditions. In response to the Protestant Reformation, the Council of Trent (1545–63) affirmed this teaching, condemning those who denied the efficacy of prayers for the dead or the use of indulgences. In the sixteenth century, Protestant Reformers vehemently opposed the Catholic practice of indulgences. The Reformers viewed indulgences as a corrupt distortion of the biblical teaching on grace, repentance, and forgiveness. Martin Luther's *Ninety-five Theses* (1517) famously challenged the Catholic Church's sale of indulgences by criticizing the claim that forgiveness of sins or reduction of purgatorial punishment could be obtained through financial contributions. The Council of Trent, however, reaffirmed the validity of indulgences stating that the Church, by virtue of the authority given to it by Christ, has the power to grant them. The council upheld their theological foundation as rooted in the communion of saints and the treasury of merits accumulated by Christ and the saints. However, it also recognized that abuses had occurred in the granting and use of indulgences, which had caused confusion among the faithful.

In response to these concerns, the Council of Trent called for reform and careful regulation of indulgences. It decreed that all "base gain" associated with indulgences should be abolished and that Church leaders should avoid even the appearance of greed or manipulation in their distribution. The council instructed bishops to be vigilant and ensure that indulgences were not misused. This attempt at reform did not eliminate indulgences but sought to restore their use within Catholic doctrine. These decisions are reflected in the *Decree on Indulgences* promulgated on December 4, 1563. The decree states:

> Whereas the power of conferring indulgences was granted by Christ to the Church; and she has, even in the most ancient times, used the said power, delivered unto her by God, the sacred and

---

5. Aquinas, *Summa Theologiae* Suppl., Q71.

holy Synod teaches and enjoins that the use of indulgences, most salutary for the Christian people and approved of by the authority of sacred councils, is to be retained in the Church; and it condemns with anathema those who either assert that they are useless or who deny that there is in the Church the power of granting them. But moderation and discretion in the use of them must be observed; and in regard to that corruption of selling indulgences (*purgantium venditio*), which is extremely scandalous to all Christendom, that must be utterly abolished; and the most diligent care must be taken that in the administering of them all abuse, superstition, and slavish servitude be avoided.[6]

Further, the CCC states, "The Church also commends almsgiving, indulgences, and works of penance undertaken on behalf of the dead" (CCC 1032). This belief highlights communal salvation where the faithful on earth (the Church Militant), the souls in purgatory (the Church Suffering), and the saints in heaven (the Church Triumphant) are spiritually united.

BIBLICAL RESPONSE TO THE DOCTRINE OF PURGATORY

A biblical critique of purgatory focuses on the following arguments: (1) the sufficiency of Christ's atonement, (2) the clarity of eternal destinations after death, and (3) the absence of clear biblical teaching about purgatory.

First, Scripture emphasizes the full and final nature of Christ's sacrifice. Hebrews 10:14 states, "For by a single offering he has perfected for all time those who are being sanctified." The idea that believers require further purification undermines the efficacy of Christ's atonement once for all (1 John 1:7). Second, the New Testament consistently presents death as leading directly to one's eternal destiny. In Luke 16:19–31 (the account of the rich man and Lazarus), both individuals are immediately taken to their respective places in the spiritual realm. There is no indication of an intermediate state for purification. Third, the verses often used to support purgatory support the doctrine only vaguely. For example, Protestants would argue that 2 Macc 12:45 is not part of the canon of Scripture and thus cannot be used to establish doctrine. While that issue is beyond the scope of this chapter, 1 Cor 3:13–15 speaks of testing by fire, but the context is the judgment of works, not souls. The passage addresses rewards, not purification. It is unclear whether the phrase "it will be revealed by fire" describes

---

6. Council of Trent, *Decree on Indulgences*, 230–31.

the "Day" (i.e., the subject of the previous clause) or each one's work (i.e., the subject of the clause before that). The translation "[will] be punished" is given here by BDAG.[7] But the next clause says "he will be delivered" and so "suffering loss" is more likely to refer to the destruction of the "work" by fire or the loss of the reward that could have been gained. Matthew 12:32 discusses the unpardonable sin, but its implication about forgiveness "in the age to come" cannot establish purgatory as a definite reality. In context, the age to come is the age when Jesus returns for his church. The issue is not about salvation through purgatory but condemnation.

SANCTIFICATION AS A COMPLETED PROCESS

Romans 8:1 declares, "There is therefore now no condemnation for those who are in Christ Jesus." The biblical picture of salvation includes justification, sanctification, and glorification—but the Scriptures speak of believers as already sanctified (1 Cor 6:11) and seated with Christ (Eph 2:6). While believers continue to grow in holiness in this life (2 Pet 1:5–8), Scripture presents the transformation after death as immediate.

Ephesians 2:8–9 states, "For by grace you have been saved through faith, and this is not your own doing; it is the gift of God, not a result of works, so that no one may boast." The doctrine of purgatory, particularly when linked with indulgences and prayers for the dead, introduces a works-based element into the economy of salvation. If Christ's work is sufficient, and salvation is a gift, then no purgatorial suffering is necessary. Paul writes in Phil 1:23 that he desires "to depart and be with Christ, for that is far better." Paul never pleas for purgatory even as the greatest of sinners (1 Tim 1:15). Paul wanted to enjoy the immediacy of being in the spiritual realm.

CONCLUSION

While the Catholic doctrine of purgatory has a long tradition, supported by the magisterium and some early church fathers, it lacks biblical support. The sufficiency of Christ's atonement, the immediacy of post-death destinations, and the biblical teachings on justification and sanctification by the blood of Jesus call the doctrine into question. From a biblical perspective, purgatory appears as an unnecessary and unbiblical addition to the gospel message. Put simply, purgatory is not scriptural.

7. BDAG, s.v. ζημιόω 2.

11

Relics

Rooted in the early history of Christianity and tied closely to Catholicism's understanding of the communion of saints, relics are honored in Catholicism as physical objects associated with the saints that mediate grace. This chapter explores the doctrine of relics as found in the official teaching of the Catholic Church and its historical tradition, considers their development and function in the life of the Catholic Church, and offers a biblical response that questions the theological necessity and biblical warrant for the veneration of relics.

CATHOLIC DOCTRINE OF RELICS

The CCC does not offer an extensive doctrinal statement on relics but does affirm the veneration of saints and their remains as part of the broader communion of saints.

> By canonizing some of the faithful, i.e., by solemnly proclaiming that they practiced heroic virtue and lived in fidelity to God's grace, the Church recognizes the power of the Spirit of holiness within her and sustains the hope of believers by proposing the saints to them as models and intercessors (CCC 828).

> Being more closely united to Christ, those who dwell in heaven fix the whole Church more firmly in holiness.... They do not cease to intercede with the Father for us (CCC 956).

Although these references emphasize intercession, the veneration of relics is historically justified by the Catholic Church as a way of honoring the saint. A Vatican document entitled the *Directory on Popular Piety and the Liturgy* (2001) more explicitly affirms relics by stating, "The relics of the Saints are properly venerated by the faithful, and authentic relics should be preserved and honored with dignity."[1] Relics are often displayed in altars, used in processions, and considered instruments of grace by proximity.

HISTORICAL DEVELOPMENT OF THE DOCTRINE OF RELICS

Relic veneration began as early as the second century. The Martyrdom of Polycarp (ca. 156 AD) describes Christians collecting his bones and treating them as "more valuable than precious stones and finer than gold" (Martyrdom of Polycarp 18.2).

In the fourth century, as Christianity became legalized in the Roman Empire, relics became common in churches. Ambrose (d. 397) discovered the relics of Saints Gervasius and Protasius and claimed miracles occurred at their tomb.[2] Jerome (d. 420) encouraged the veneration of relics, though he clarified that Christians do not adore the relics but venerate them to honor the saints.[3]

A more structured theology of relics developed in the Middle Ages where relics were considered powerful instruments of healing and protection. Pilgrimages to relic sites became popular and cathedrals were constructed to house them. The Council of Trent (1545–63), which was formed to respond to Protestant criticism, reaffirmed the veneration of relics. It stated, "Also, that the holy bodies of holy martyrs and of others now living with Christ . . . are to be venerated by the faithful, for through these [bodies] many benefits are bestowed by God on men."[4] Relics ultimately became sacramentals—i.e., ob-

---

1. Congregation for Divine Worship and the Discipline of the Sacraments, *Directory on Popular Piety* §236.
2. Mershman, "Sts. Gervasius and Protasius."
3. Jerome, "Letter 46 (to Oceanus)," 420.
4. Council of Trent, *Decree on Indulgences*, 230–31.

jects that do not confer grace as sacraments do but that prepare individuals to receive grace through the right disposition and faith.

The Catholic Church classifies relics into three types. First-class relics are physical body parts of a saint (e.g., bone, hair, blood). Second-class relics are items used or worn by the saint during life (e.g., clothing, rosary). Finally, third-class relics are objects touched to a first-class relic (e.g., cloth). Relics are often embedded in altars or reliquaries, and are frequently used in special feast days or blessings. These objects are believed to be conduits of God's grace due to the sanctity of the individual with whom they are associated.

Catholic theology defends relics based on four primary principles. First is the sanctity of the body. Since the body is the temple of the Holy Spirit (1 Cor 6:19), the bodies of saints—who were particularly holy—retain special dignity. Second is the incarnational principle, which states that God works through material things (e.g., water, bread, wine). Third is the communion of saints. The unity of the Church on earth and in heaven means the faithful may honor the saints and benefit from their intercession, including through their physical remains. Fourth is historical precedent in which the long-standing practice of the Church is used to justify the theological legitimacy of relics.

A BIBLICAL RESPONSE TO THE DOCTRINE OF RELICS

The veneration of relics raises several theological concerns. These include the risk of idolatry, the nature of Christ's mediation, and the sufficiency of Scripture and Christ's work. There is no direct biblical command to venerate relics. While Scripture records instances of God using physical objects for miraculous purposes—such as Elisha's bones bringing a man back to life (2 Kgs 13:21) or Paul's handkerchief healing the sick (Acts 19:11–12)—these are descriptive, not prescriptive. The Bible never instructs believers to collect, venerate, or pray in the presence of objects. The danger lies in extrapolating doctrine from isolated miracles rather than from sustained theological teaching.

The veneration of relics can blur the line between honor and worship. Exodus 20:4–5 prohibits making or bowing before images or objects in religious devotion. As previously noted, while Catholic theology distinguishes *latria* (worship due to God) from *dulia* (honor given to saints), the practice often resembles the kind of object-centered devotion condemned in Scripture. For example, Paul writes in Rom 1:25, "They exchanged the truth about God for a lie and worshiped and served the creature rather than the Creator." The Reformers of the sixteenth century were deeply concerned that relics promoted superstition and distracted from true faith in Christ.[5]

As noted in many chapters previously, 1 Tim 2:5 emphasizes the exclusivity of Christ's intercession. The idea that touching or being near the bones or clothing of saints can bring healing or favor introduces a form of mediation that Scripture does not support. Moreover, the book of Hebrews repeatedly teaches that believers have direct access to God through Christ (Heb 4:14–16; 10:19–22). Venerating relics suggests that divine grace is mediated through other humans or their belongings rather than through Christ alone.

The New Testament moves the emphasis of worship away from physical locations and objects. Jesus tells the Samaritan woman at the well, "The hour is coming when neither on this mountain nor in Jerusalem will you worship the Father.... True worshipers will worship the Father in spirit and truth" (John 4:21–24). The gospel of Christ emphasizes a heart-centered faith. The necessity of relics does not fit with this call for worship. Salvation and blessing come through Christ alone. Romans 5:1 states, "Therefore, since we have been justified by faith, we have peace with God through our Lord Jesus Christ." Using relics to secure favor with God shifts one's trust away from the finished work of Christ to material intermediaries.

History shows numerous examples of fake, commercialized, and manipulated relics. This abuse led to Martin Luther's criticism, "It is not necessary to believe in any relic, and it is better not to believe."[6] By the time of the Protestant Reformation, there were so many alleged pieces of the "True Cross" of Jesus that John Calvin remarked they could build a ship with them.[7]

CONCLUSION

The doctrine of relics arises from a theology that values the body, tradition, and the visible communion of saints. While it seeks to honor God's work in holy men and women, it introduces practices not found in Scripture and susceptible to misunderstanding. The biblical response emphasizes the all-sufficiency of Christ, the inward and spiritual nature of worship, and

---

5. Calvin, *Treatise on Relics*, 221–23.
6. Luther, *Table Talk*, 446.
7. Calvin, *Treatise on Relics*, 302.

the sole mediatorship of Jesus. Christians are never called to seek grace through objects. Instead, Christians must draw near to God through faith in Christ. Relics may have historical interest, but they should not be objects of spiritual veneration.

12

The Eucharist

THE EUCHARIST, ALSO CALLED the Lord's Supper or Holy Communion, is one of the most sacred and debated practices in the Christian faith. Among Christian traditions, few doctrines carry such theological weight and divergent interpretation. While nearly all branches of Christianity observe the Eucharist in some form, nearly all branches differ in what they believe is happening during the rite. For the Roman Catholic Church, the Eucharist is not merely symbolic—it is a sacrament in which the bread and wine become the actual body and blood of Jesus Christ. This transformation is known as "transubstantiation" and reflects the true presence of Christ in the rite. However, many Protestants and other non-Catholic Christians challenge this view. This chapter explores the Catholic doctrine of the Eucharist—particularly its affirmation of transubstantiation—then presents a response rooted in Scripture and early church interpretation.

In Catholic theology, the Eucharist (from the Greek *eucharistō* meaning "to give thanks") occupies a central and exalted place in the liturgy. The CCC defines the Eucharist as "the source and summit of the Christian life" (CCC 1324). According to official Catholic teaching, Christ himself is truly, really, and substantially present in the Eucharist. At the consecration during the Mass, the bread and wine are believed to change into the literal body and blood of Christ, even though the physical appearance of bread and wine remain. The term *transubstantiation* draws from Aristotelian metaphysics. The distinction made is between "substance," the underlying reality, and "accidents," the observable characteristics. The Council of Trent formalized this understanding in response to the Protestant Reformation, declaring, "By the consecration of the bread and wine, a conversion is made of the whole substance of the bread into the substance of the body of Christ our Lord, and of the whole substance of the wine into the substance of his blood . . . which conversion the holy Catholic Church most aptly calls Transubstantiation" (Council of Trent, Session XIII, Canon II).

Supporters of the doctrine often appeal to Scripture for validation. Among the most cited passages is John 6:53–56, where Jesus says, "Unless you eat the flesh of the Son of Man and drink his blood, you have no life in you. . . . For my flesh is real food and my blood is real drink." Catholics interpret this passage literally by maintaining that Christ's language indicates a necessary consumption of his actual body and blood. Likewise, at the Last Supper, Jesus took bread, gave thanks, broke it, and said, "This is my body," and concerning the cup, "This is my blood of the covenant, which is poured out for many for the forgiveness of sins" (Matt 26:26–28). Catholic theologians argue that Jesus's words should be taken at face value, which form the theological foundation for the belief that the elements truly become Christ's body and blood.

Historically, there is evidence that early Christians affirmed a real presence in the Eucharist, though the specifics vary. Ignatius of Antioch, writing around AD 110, stated that heretics "abstain from the Eucharist and from prayer, because they do not confess that the Eucharist is the flesh of our Savior Jesus Christ" (Ignatius, *Letter to the Smyrnaeans* 7.1). Justin Martyr, around AD 150, similarly wrote, "We do not receive these as common bread and common drink; but . . . we have been taught that the food . . . is the flesh and blood of that Jesus who was made flesh" (Justin Martyr, *First Apology* 66). While these statements affirm a strong belief in the real presence of Christ in the Eucharist, they do not necessarily affirm transubstantiation as later defined. The early church often embraced mystery without the philosophical precision that was to come later.

It wasn't until the Middle Ages that the doctrine of transubstantiation was fully developed and codified. Around the eleventh century, theologians like Lanfranc and later Thomas Aquinas provided systematic articulation using Aristotelian categories. Aquinas wrote in the *Summa Theologiae*, "The body of Christ is in this sacrament not after the manner of a body, but by the mode of substance."[1] The Fourth Lateran Council in 1215 formally

---

1. Aquinas, *Summa Theologiae* 3, Q75, A1.

used the term "transubstantiated" to describe the change, and the Council of Trent would later reaffirm it in the face of Protestant dissent.[2]

On the other hand, the Protestant Reformers strongly objected to this doctrine. Even so, Martin Luther, the instigator of the Reformation, maintained a belief in the real presence of Christ in the Eucharist but rejected transubstantiation. He proposed a view sometimes called "consubstantiation," in which Christ is present "in, with, and under" the bread and wine.[3] Ulrich Zwingli, by contrast, saw the Eucharist as an entirely symbolic memorial of Christ's death.[4] John Calvin struck a middle path by arguing for a spiritual presence where the faithful are united with Christ spiritually but not physically in the elements.[5] These perspectives were shaped by a shared concern to return to the biblical witness and to avoid what they perceived as superstition or idolatry in Catholic eucharistic devotion.

From a biblical standpoint, several key objections can be raised to the doctrine of transubstantiation. First, the interpretation of John 6 must be examined in its full context. While Jesus says in vv. 53–56 that his followers must eat his flesh and drink his blood, he also clarifies in v. 63, "It is the Spirit who gives life; the flesh is of no avail. The words that I have spoken to you are spirit and life." Earlier in the discourse, Jesus identified himself as the bread of life and equated coming to him and believing in him with eating and drinking (John 6:35). This suggests a metaphorical reading. Thus, to "eat his flesh" is to believe in him deeply and personally. The misunderstanding of the crowd in John 6:52—"How can this man give us his flesh to eat?"—parallels other episodes in John's Gospel where Jesus's metaphors are misunderstood as literal (cf. John 3:4; 4:11).

Further, the words of institution at the Last Supper are more reasonably understood symbolically. When Jesus said, "This is my body," his literal body was present before the disciples. He had not yet been crucified, and his blood had not yet been shed. This suggests he was speaking figuratively, as he often did. Jesus frequently spoke metaphorically of himself and his role. For example, Jesus said things like, "I am the vine," "I am the door," and "I am the Good Shepherd." To insist on a literal interpretation here while acknowledging figurative language elsewhere is inconsistent. Additionally, the context of the Passover meal reinforces the symbolic nature of

---

2. Tanner, "Fourth Lateran Council, 1215," 232–67.
3. Luther, *Large Catechism*, 420–30.
4. McGrath, *Reformation Thought*, 142.
5. Calvin, *Institutes* 3.18.1–4.

the Eucharist. Just as the original Passover was a memorial of God's deliverance from Egypt (cf. Exod 12), the Lord's Supper is a memorial of Christ's redemptive death. Paul affirms this in 1 Cor 11:26 when he writes, "For as often as you eat this bread and drink the cup, you proclaim the Lord's death until he comes." The act is a proclamation of Christ's death, not a literal repetition or reenactment of his sacrifice.

The Epistle to the Hebrews offers perhaps the most compelling biblical rebuttal to transubstantiation. Hebrews repeatedly emphasizes that Christ's sacrifice was once for all. Hebrews 10:10 states, "We have been sanctified through the offering of the body of Jesus Christ once for all." Later the author writes, "When Christ had offered for all time a single sacrifice for sins, he sat down at the right hand of God" (Heb 10:12), and, "There is no longer any offering for sin" (Heb 10:18). This language directly opposes any notion that Christ is sacrificed anew in each Mass, whether "unbloody" or otherwise. The repeated performance of the sacrifice in practice undermines the finality of the cross emphasized in Scripture.

Practical concerns also arise. The Catholic practice of eucharistic adoration—worshiping the consecrated host as the real presence of Christ—raises serious questions about idolatry. Scripture is clear in its prohibition of worshiping created things (cf. Exod 20:4–5). If the host is not truly Christ, then such worship is idolatrous. Furthermore, Paul's instructions about the Lord's Supper in 1 Cor 11 emphasize worthy participation in the community, warning against greed, division, and self-exaltation, yet mentions nothing against failure to believe in transubstantiation. The danger lay in treating the meal casually and selfishly, not in misunderstanding metaphysical doctrine.

A NON-PROTESTANT, NON-CATHOLIC VIEW

Unlike many Protestant denominations which observe Communion monthly, quarterly, or on special occasions, there are some Christians who believe that the Lord's Supper should be observed every Sunday without exception. This conviction is grounded in the church's understanding of New Testament precedent, early church practice, and the theological purpose of Communion itself. The foundation for this practice lies first in the apostolic example found in the book of Acts. In Acts 20:7, Luke records, "On the first day of the week, when we were gathered together to break bread, Paul talked with them until midnight." This brief statement reveals several important details. First, it establishes that the Christians in Troas had a regular meeting on the first day of the week. Second, the stated purpose of their gathering was "to break bread," a term widely understood by biblical scholars and early Christian writers to refer to the Lord's Supper (cf. Acts 2:42, 46).[6]

In 1 Cor 11, Paul provides extensive instruction concerning the Lord's Supper by rebuking the Corinthians for their abuses and reminding them of its meaning. Paul quotes Jesus's words at the Last Supper when he writes, "Do this in remembrance of me" (1 Cor 11:24–25). While the frequency is not specified in that passage, Paul later connects their partaking of the Supper to their regular assembly. He writes "when you come together as a church" in v. 18, and again, "When you come together to eat, wait for one another" in v. 33. These statements imply that the Lord's Supper was a regular part of their communal worship. Notably, in 1 Cor 16:1–2, Paul gives instructions about giving contributions "on the first day of every week," confirming that the Corinthian church gathered each Sunday. It is highly unlikely they would assemble every Sunday only for giving. Instead, we can infer that they gathered to observe the Lord's Supper, read Scripture, and pray just as those in Troas.

To be sure, the Lord's Supper is more than a ritual—it is an act of communion with Christ and with one another. Paul writes, "The cup of blessing that we bless, is it not a participation (*koinōnia*) in the blood of Christ? The bread that we break, is it not a participation (*koinōnia*) in the body of Christ?" (1 Cor 10:16). The Greek word *koinōnia* denotes deep relational fellowship. The Supper is therefore not a passive remembering, but an active communion with the crucified and risen Lord. This ongoing participation should be a continual part of the Christian's life, and the first day of the week—the day Christ rose from the dead (cf. Mark 16:9)—is the biblically prescribed time for this act of resurrection remembrance.

Early Christian writings support the weekly observance of the Lord's Supper, if not more frequently. The Didache, a late-first-century or early-second-century Christian manual, refers to the Eucharist as a recurring event and offers prayers for its administration (Didache 9–10). More explicitly, Justin Martyr describes the Christian worship assembly in his *First Apology*.

> And on the day called Sunday, all who live in cities or in the country gather together to one place, and the memoirs of the apostles or the writings of the prophets are read, as long as time

---

6. Bruce, *Book of the Acts*, 174.

permits; then, when the reader has ceased, the president verbally instructs, and exhorts to the imitation of these good things. Then we all rise together and pray, and, as we before said, when our prayer is ended, bread and wine and water are brought, and the president in like manner offers prayers and thanksgivings, according to his ability, and the people assent, saying, Amen; and there is a distribution to each, and a participation of that over which thanks have been given, and to those who are absent a portion is sent by the deacons. And those who are well to do, and willing, give what each thinks fit; and what is collected is deposited with the president, who succours the orphans and widows, and those who, through sickness or any other cause, are in want, and those who are in bonds, and the strangers sojourning among us, and in a word takes care of all who are in need. But Sunday is the day on which we all hold our common assembly, because it is the first day on which God, having wrought a change in the darkness and matter, made the world, and Jesus Christ our savior on the same day rose from the dead. For he was crucified on the day before that of Saturn [Saturday]; and on the day after that of Saturn, which is the day of the Sun [Sunday], having appeared to his apostles and disciples, he taught them those things, which we have submitted for your consideration.[7]

Sunday worship and the observance of the Supper were tightly interconnected throughout the earliest centuries of the church.

Leaders of the American Restoration Movement such as Thomas Campbell, Alexander Campbell, and Barton W. Stone advocated that Christians should do in the present what the apostles and earliest churches did in the New Testament era. Alexander Campbell, in his debate with Presbyterian minister W. L. MacCalla in 1823, stated, "There is neither precept nor example in the New Testament for keeping the Lord's Supper quarterly or annually. The primitive disciples met on the first day of every week to break bread, and every Lord's day is a memorial of the resurrection of Jesus."[8]

In addition to scriptural and historical foundations, there are strong theological reasons to partake of the Lord's Supper weekly. Each Sunday, believers are commanded to remember the cross and thereby proclaim the Lord's death (1 Cor 11:26), thus reaffirming their unity in Christ's body. In a world of distraction and doctrinal drift, this regular anchoring in the death, burial, and resurrection of Jesus is vital. Weekly observance protects

---

7. Justin Martyr, *First Apology*, in *ANF* 1:186.
8. See Campbell, "Address on the Lord's Supper," 97.

against both neglect and overemphasis. Infrequent observance can lead the Lord's Supper to become an occasional ritual that is disconnected from the rhythm of Christian life. On the other hand, weekly practice makes it ordinary without making it trivial. Like prayer or the reading of Scripture, the Lord's Supper becomes a weekly pattern that shapes Christian identity.

However, some might object, suggesting that weekly observance diminishes its significance by making it routine and thereby less sacred. However, repetition does not necessarily lead to meaninglessness. Worship, prayer, preaching, and giving are weekly practices in most congregations, yet their frequency does not reduce their spiritual value. In fact, regularity can enhance reverence when approached thoughtfully and with spiritual preparation.

Moreover, the Lord's Supper promotes congregational unity. As Paul emphasized, "Because there is one bread, we who are many are one body, for we all partake of the one bread" (1 Cor 10:17). Weekly participation reminds the local congregation that their shared life is rooted not in common interest, politics, or social status, but in the crucified Christ. In an increasingly fragmented and individualistic culture, this communal meal declares the unity of the people of God.

Partaking of the Lord's Supper every Sunday is a faithful response to the apostolic pattern. It is a continuation of early Christian worship and is an act of communion with Christ and his body. The weekly taking of the Lord's Supper proclaims the death of Jesus, remembers his resurrection, anticipates his return, and unites believers in his body. The Lord's Supper is a weekly encounter with grace, memory, and fellowship. It is an anchor for faith and worship every Lord's Day without having to crucify Christ over again.

CONCLUSION

The Roman Catholic doctrine of transubstantiation is a theological system that developed over centuries and is built on philosophical assumptions not found in Scripture. Though it aims to honor Christ's presence in the Eucharist, it imposes metaphysical categories foreign to the biblical text. A careful reading of relevant passages such as John 6, the Synoptic accounts of the Last Supper, 1 Cor 11, and Heb 10 reveals a consistent message—the Eucharist is a memorial, a proclamation, and a spiritual act of communion with Christ. It is not a literal re-sacrificing or reincarnation of his flesh and blood. It cannot be if the book of Hebrews is infallible. The early church's affirmation of Christ's presence in the Eucharist should be respected but need not require belief in transubstantiation. The power of the Eucharist lies in the shared remembrance of Christ's once-for-all atonement and the unity of the body of believers.

13

Where I Stand With Catholicism

THE WORD "CATHOLIC" MEANS "universal." That much is true, and that much I can get behind. Scripture is clear that there is one true, universal body of Christ and that body is the church. A person is either in Christ's body (the church) or not. The idea of denominations (or "Christianities," plural) makes no sense from a New Testament perspective. To that end, I must agree with my Catholic friends. There is one church. It is the body of Christ. It began fifty days after the crucifixion of Jesus on the day of Pentecost in Jerusalem and has continued in its existence until the modern day. As our Lord said, "The gates of Hades will not overtake it" (Matt 16:18). Thus, I affirm that any true Christian must accept that he or she is part of the one "catholic" church. Notice, however, that in this rendering, the term "catholic" is lowercased. I am not suggesting that a Christian must undergo RCIA (Rite of Christian Initiation of Adults) training, nor am I suggesting that the Roman capital-"C" Catholic Church is the *true* church of Jesus. I am only stating the biblical truth that there is one church, and this one church is universal and belongs to Christ.

I further agree that one only enters the church via baptism into the body of Christ. This teaching is clear from passages such as Acts 2:38, 22:16, 1 Pet 3:21, and Jesus's own words to Nicodemus in John 3:5—"unless one is born of water and spirit"—which, according to all the earliest church fathers, refers to baptism. Though I did not address this issue in the previous chapters, I do reject the doctrine of infant baptism that is popular among

Where I Stand With Catholicism

Catholics. Baptism in the New Testament occurs when one comes to faith in Christ. Baptism is performed immediately and administered only to those who believe. Children, especially infants, do not have the capacity for personal faith. Unfortunately, the intricacies of this issue must be reserved for another time. Most Protestants reject or diminish the sacramental life of the church; yet, Catholicism reminds us that baptism and the Eucharist (i.e., Lord's Supper or Communion) put us in and maintain our relationship with God in Christ.

Though I have demonstrated some doctrinal and theological failings of Catholicism in the previous chapters, I appreciate the Catholic Church. Few religious institutions have done as much (likely not more) to combat the needs of our world. Catholics build hospitals and children's homes. Catholics serve as activists against the evils of abortion, gender issues, and sexual ethics. The pope is perhaps the most influential human alive. While I obviously disagree theologically with many significant tenets of Catholicism, that does not mean I disapprove of the good they are doing in the world.

I am typing this section just after the election of Pope Leo XIV. After the death of Pope Francis, the world paused as the conclave of cardinals conferred to elect the new leader of the Catholic Church. The world held its breath as black smoke would rise from the Sistine Chapel until finally white smoke appeared, declaring a successful election and the coming appointing of the new pope.

It was at this time that my wife and I were critically thinking about why we are not Catholic. We both enjoy Catholic podcasts and appreciate Catholic activists. I recall one YouTuber who converted to Catholicism from Pentecostalism saying, "One day I just had to ask myself, 'Why am I not Catholic?'" The explorations of this question led him to convert to Catholicism. He, like many in Protestant circles, struggled with doctrines of Mary, the saints, the pope, etc. For this man (who is a PhD historian), the writings and statements of the church fathers and the saints—whether properly rooted in Scripture or not—were enough to convince him. It seems to me that the issue surrounding the Catholic/Protestant debate is that for Catholics to convert to Protestantism, they must reject what they currently affirm, while for Protestants to convert to Catholicism, they must affirm what they currently reject. In this sense, Catholicism typically finds itself on the offensive side of the court while Protestantism stands on the defensive.

Section One

My view, as I have demonstrated in the previous chapters, is not to affirm or reject the doctrines of men but to critically explore Scripture. If I cannot find good biblical precedence for a doctrine, I cannot accept that doctrine. This is different from the doctrine of *sola scriptura*. I am not looking for "thou shall" or "thou shall not" statements in Scripture. Instead, I am asking if the text allows for such teachings. As David Instone-Brewer rightly notes:

> We have a better chance of understanding the New Testament in its original context than did the second-century church fathers. We have a greater knowledge of the language and culture of the first century than they did, partly because we can have a more accurate perspective on the changes that happened by looking at them from a distance.[1]

To that end, there are places in which I have been neglectful, primarily in my view of Mary and the Eucharist. As stated above, I reject the notion of praying to Mary, and I reject the worship of any being or thing other that the triune Godhead. However, when the pregnant Mary came to her cousin, Elizabeth became filled with the Holy Spirit and exclaimed, "Blessed are you among women!" (Luke 1:42). I find in Protestant circles, Mary is often viewed as nothing more than the vessel for Christ's entrance into the world. Though I reject the Immaculate Conception (i.e., the doctrine that Mary was born sinless) and Mary's perpetual virginity, Mary is truly blessed among women. She should hold honor and respect in the church of Jesus Christ in the same way that the church honors and respects Paul as an apostle. The church should honor and respect Mary for her role in birthing, raising, and shaping the life of Jesus while he was on the earth.

Additionally, the Eucharist has always been important to me. It is clear from Scripture that the earliest Christians met to partake of the Lord's Supper and that some of them partook of it inappropriately (e.g., the Corinthians; cf. 1 Cor 11:17–22). Given the scriptural parameters and promises regarding the Lord's Supper, Christians should see the presence of Jesus *with* the Eucharist rather than *in* the Eucharist. To be sure, the Lord's Supper is not just a symbol. As Flannery O'Connor said, "Well, if it's a symbol, to hell with it."[2] However, when read in context, Scripture does not substantiate transubstantiation.

---

1. Instone-Brewer, *Divorce and Remarriage*, 149.
2. O'Connor, *Habit of Being*, 100.

Where I Stand With Catholicism

So, why am I not Roman Catholic? The only truly infallible authority in the church is Jesus Christ and divinely inspired Scripture. The Catholic Church teaches that the pope and the magisterium have qualities of divinity that I am not willing to accept. Additionally, matters of Mary, the saints, and the authority of Tradition have no root in the New Testament church of the first century.

Though I am not Roman Catholic, I certainly am "catholic." Again, I must emphasize the lowercased "c" as referring to the one true, universal church. There is one church. We are either in it, or we are not. Although I am not convinced that the Roman Catholic Church is it, there is one true catholic church—the body of Christ. If it is not in Catholicism, can it be found in Protestantism and more narrowly in Calvinistic doctrines? I will explore this in the next section.

SECTION TWO

Agreement and Disagreement with the Protestant Reformation and Calvinism

14

The Good and the Bad of the Protestant Reformation

THE PROTESTANT REFORMATION STANDS as one of the most transformative movements in Christian history. Sparked in the early sixteenth century by figures such as Martin Luther, Ulrich Zwingli, and John Calvin, the Reformation was fueled by a desire to correct abuses and doctrinal errors in the Roman Catholic Church, namely regarding the selling of relics and the doctrine of penance. After his study of the doctrines of grace and faith, Luther's disgust with relics and penance led to his rejection of the veneration of relics, a renewed emphasis on the authority of Scripture alone, and the translation of the Bible into the common languages of the people. These reforms were instrumental in empowering lay Christians.

Even with its good, the Reformation also introduced theological shifts that merit scrutiny—most notably, the doctrine of *sola gratia*, or "grace alone," and *sola fide*, or "faith alone," which has often been interpreted in ways that diminish the role of obedience, baptism, and discipleship. This chapter examines both the commendable achievements and the critical weaknesses of the Protestant Reformation.

Section Two

THE REFORMATION'S BREAK FROM RELICS

One of the most significant contributions of the Protestant Reformation was its sharp critique of the Roman Catholic Church's use of relics and associated superstitions. During the late medieval period, the Catholic Church venerated relics such as purported fragments of the cross, bones of saints, and pieces of the Virgin Mary's clothing. These objects were believed to possess miraculous powers. Churches housing relics became pilgrimage sites that drew financial contributions and spiritual prestige.

Additionally, the Catholic Church taught that the purchase of relics could free loved ones from purgatory. The Dominican friar Johann Tetzel (who was a contemporary of Martin Luther) is often attributed with the saying, "As soon as a coin in the coffer rings, a soul from purgatory springs." His purpose in selling relics was to raise money for the building of a massive cathedral. Tetzel perfected fear-buying. His powerful speeches would emphasize the burning pains of hell and the difficulty of purgatory. The cure? Buy a relic and save not only your soul but the souls of those you love. Salvation as proclaimed by Tetzel and others during the sixteenth century was not the result of Christ's work on the cross and his resurrection but works of pseudo-righteousness for monetary gain.

The Reformers denounced such practices as unscriptural and idolatrous. In his *Ninety-five Theses* (1517), Luther challenged the theological basis for the veneration of relics and indulgences by arguing that salvation could not be bought or mediated through physical objects. Instead, he emphasized a direct relationship between the believer and God through faith and Scripture. Although Luther does not rebuke relics directly, theses 27 and 52 are of great importance to his views.[1]

> Thesis 27: "They preach only human doctrines who say that as soon as the money clinks into the money chest, the soul flies out of purgatory."
>
> Thesis 52: "It is vain to trust in salvation by indulgence letters, even though the indulgence commissary, or even the pope, were to offer his own soul as security."

This objection and later rejection of relics helped refocus Christian worship away from the material. It restored the primacy of Christ's once-for-all sacrifice and challenged the ecclesiastical structures that profited

---

1. Luther, *Disputation*, 31–33.

from superstition. By stripping away these layers, the Reformation called Christians back to a more biblical form of worship centered on the doctrines found in Scripture.

BIBLE TRANSLATIONS AND THE RISE OF THE BIBLE IN THE COMMON VERNACULAR

A second monumental achievement of the Reformation was its commitment to translating the Bible from Jerome's Latin Vulgate (as it had been received in the Western church as the authoritative text) into common languages such as German and English. While Latin was the language of the educated ecclesial elite, it was incomprehensible to most Christians. This linguistic barrier placed Scripture under the control of clergy, making the laity dependent on their interpretations. Because the laity could not read Latin, they could not read the Bible for themselves. Thus, when a priest said one must offer ten Our Fathers for penance, for example, they had to trust what was being said.

While the Vulgate was a great tool that brought the Hebrew and Greek Scriptures into a language readable for that time (ca. 405), Jerome did not offer the best glosses in his translation. One such rendering led to massive false teaching until William Tyndale corrected it with his translation. Jerome supplied the Latin gloss *paenitentia* ("do penance") for the Greek term *metanoeō* ("to repent"). Jerome's term emphasized doing works to undo the wrong that had been committed. However, the original Greek term only means to change one's mind, i.e., to decide to refrain from sin from that moment on by asking for forgiveness and live according to the standard of Christ.

The apostolic message of the gospel had always been one of clear proclamation. Pentecost itself (cf. Acts 2) affirms the importance of linguistic accessibility. The Holy Spirit empowered the apostles to preach the gospel in the native languages of its hearers. In this light, the Reformation rightly reclaimed the importance of understanding and internalizing Scripture. Reformers like Luther in Germany, Tyndale in England, and later Calvin in Geneva insisted that Scripture be accessible to all believers. Luther's German Bible (1522–34) and Tyndale's English New Testament (1526) were revolutionary. These translations empowered ordinary Christians to read, interpret, and apply Scripture for themselves. William Tyndale's translation of the Bible into English in the early sixteenth century marked a revolutionary moment in church history and the development of the English language. Tyndale believed that every Christian had the right to read the Bible in their own tongue. Tyndale famously said, "If God spare my life, ere many years, I will cause a boy that driveth the plough shall know more of the Scripture than thou dost."[2] Tyndale reportedly said this during a conversation with a learned clergyman who defended the Church's control over access to the Bible. His translation—drawn directly from Hebrew and Greek texts rather than from the Latin Vulgate—was the first English Bible to be printed using the printing press. John Wycliffe had made an English translation around 1382; however, the use of Johann Gutenberg's printing press made Tyndale's work far more accessible to the public. Tyndale's work emphasized clarity, accuracy, and readability. It laid the linguistic and theological foundation for future English translations.

Tyndale's translation was a theological and political act of defiance. He challenged the Catholic Church's control over Scripture and doctrine. His emphasis on justification by faith and the priesthood of all believers reflected key Reformation ideas. For his work, Tyndale was condemned as a heretic and ultimately executed in 1536 by being strangled to death, then burned. Even so, his legacy endured. An estimated 80–90 percent of the King James New Testament derives directly from his translation.

THE ELEVATION OF SCRIPTURE OVER TRADITION

The Reformation advanced the principle of *sola scriptura*—i.e., "Scripture alone"—as the ultimate authority in matters of faith and doctrine. This was a necessary corrective to the perceived excesses of the Roman Catholic Church, which had elevated capital-"T" "Tradition" and papal authority to a level equal to, or at times, even above, Scripture. By insisting on the primacy of the biblical text, the Reformers reoriented theological discourse around divine revelation. The rise of expository preaching, systematic theology, and the stepping away from prescribed liturgical readings all testify to the enduring value of this reform. Moreover, the principle of *sola scriptura* guarded against the encroachment of innovations that lacked biblical warrant. It equipped the Reformers with a method that could reject doctrines and practices such as purgatory, indulgences, and the infallibility of the pope that could not be found in or substantiated by Scripture. This

---

2. Tyndale, *Works of the English Reformers*, 250.

THE PROBLEMATIC EMPHASIS ON "GRACE ALONE"

Despite its many strengths, the Protestant Reformation also introduced theological formulations that, in some cases, went too far in reacting against perceived Catholic errors. Chief among these was the doctrine of *sola gratia* (i.e., "grace alone"). While the centrality of grace in salvation is indisputable, the Reformation's interpretation of this principle often veered into theological reductionism that minimized the importance of response and obedience.

In many Reformation traditions, *sola gratia* is interpreted to mean that salvation is entirely passive on the part of the believer. That is to say humans contribute nothing, not even the response of faith, to their salvation. This interpretation, influenced by Augustinian (from Augustine of Hippo, 354–430) and later Calvinist (from John Calvin, 1509–64) thought, led to the widespread belief in "irresistible grace" and "unconditional election" wherein God's saving grace acts independently of human will or decision. Martin Luther believed that human beings are utterly incapable of earning salvation through their own efforts. For Luther, salvation is a free and unearned gift from God granted solely by his grace. Luther taught that, because of original sin, all people are spiritually dead and entirely dependent on God's initiative to save. This view stood in direct contrast to the Catholic Church's teaching that grace operates in cooperation with the sacraments. For Luther, even faith itself is not a human contribution but a result of God's work through the Holy Spirit.

Luther's emphasis on grace alone shifted the focus to the believer's direct relationship with God through faith in Christ. Luther saw grace not as a substance dispensed by the Church but as God's loving disposition toward sinners made manifest in Jesus's atoning death. Ultimately, Luther's doctrine of grace reshaped Christian understanding of salvation by emphasizing the absolute sufficiency of God in redeeming the lost.

However, views that demand grace be imputed without obedience conflict with the biblical portrayal of salvation as a synergistic relationship between divine initiative and human response. Passages such as Matt 25:31–46, Acts 2:38, 1 Pet 3:21, Rom 6:3–5, and Jas 2:24 emphasize the necessity of repentance, baptism, and obedience. Far from being meritorious works, these responses are expressions of faith that align with God's gracious offer of salvation. Moreover, the New Testament repeatedly affirms that while salvation is by grace, it is not by grace alone apart from faith, baptism, and ongoing faithfulness. Jesus's own teachings (e.g., Matt 7:21; John 15:1–10) and later biblical instruction (e.g., Heb 10:26–31) present a more holistic view in which grace empowers but does not negate human responsibility. Grace is a gift. As such, it must be freely given—as God freely gave his Son (John 3:16)—*and* freely received! The doctrines of unconditional election and irresistible grace remove the possibility of free will. I will have more to say about this in later sections.

FRAGMENTATION AND DENOMINATIONALISM

Another unintended consequence of the Reformation was the fracturing of Christian unity. To be sure, Luther did not want to begin his own religious movement. As it began, Luther's goal was simply to inquire and debate these issues publicly and biblically as many preachers, scholars, and theologians do today without breaking fellowship. Even so, the break from Rome was in many respects necessary. However, the principle of individual interpretation fueled by the doctrine of *sola scriptura* led to a proliferation of denominations where each claimed to have biblical authority for their doctrines. If everyone can interpret Scripture, then who is to say which interpretation is right and which one is wrong? From Lutherans to Reformed, Anabaptists to Anglicans, and later Baptists, Methodists, Pentecostals, and countless independent churches, the Reformation unleashed a force of division within Christianity that produced doctrinal inconsistency and instability.

This outcome stands in tension with Christ's prayer for unity among his followers in John 17:20–23 and the apostolic exhortation to maintain the unity of the Spirit (cf. Eph 4:1–6). While the Reformation rightly opposed the corruption of Catholicism, it inadvertently created a theological climate in which personal interpretation superseded apostolic teaching.

A BALANCED VIEW OF THE REFORMATION

To evaluate the Protestant Reformation fairly, one must acknowledge both its historic necessity and its theological excesses. It called believers to greater fidelity to Scripture, denounced the use of relics and the doctrine of penance, and empowered believers to engage directly with Scripture. It opposed superstition (such as purgatory) and reclaimed the centrality of Christ's atonement. These are profound and enduring achievements; yet, the Reformation also introduced soteriological simplifications. In their zeal to protect divine sovereignty, the Reformers neglected the biblical emphasis on initial obedience to the gospel message in faith. The doctrine of "grace alone," when untethered from baptism, discipleship, and holiness, risks producing a form of antinomianism—i.e., a gospel without transformation.

Furthermore, the Reformation's commitment to personal interpretation also opened the floodgates to division and subjectivism. The challenge for the true church today is to retain the best of the Reformation's legacy—its love for Scripture, its Christ-centeredness, its rejection of idolatry—while correcting its excesses with a more comprehensive and biblical theology of salvation and unity.

CONCLUSION

The Protestant Reformation was a watershed event in Christian history. It restored the authority of Scripture, encouraged religious literacy, and corrected many abuses of medieval Catholicism. Its insistence on grace, faith, and the centrality of Christ brought needed reform. At the same time, its overreaction to Catholic doctrine led to some significant theological imbalances. A mature Christian theology must learn from both the strengths and weaknesses of the Reformation by embracing its passion for biblical truth while resisting its tendencies toward reductionism and division. Only then can the true people of God faithfully continue the work of reformation in every generation.

15

Luther and Grace

THE PROTESTANT REFORMATION'S RALLYING cry of *sola gratia* ("grace alone") emerged through the theological vision of Martin Luther. A former Augustinian monk, Luther revolutionized Western Christianity by challenging the Roman Catholic system of grace mediated through relics and the sacraments. His soteriology centered on the unmerited favor of God offered freely through faith in Jesus Christ. In doing so, Luther initiated a paradigm shift in the doctrine of salvation that resounds to this day.

This chapter examines Luther's doctrine of grace as articulated in his major writings by situating it within the late-medieval context and tracing its development alongside his critique of Roman Catholic theology. It then evaluates the theological implications of *sola gratia* for the Christian life. Finally, the chapter offers a response which shares many of Luther's concerns yet remains distinct in its understanding of grace's relationship to baptism and obedience.

LUTHER AND GRACE

To understand Luther's doctrine of grace, one must first understand the context of late-medieval soteriology. By the fifteenth century, the Roman Catholic Church had developed a synergistic model of salvation in which grace and merit were interwoven. The Catholic Church taught that the initial grace of justification was imparted at baptism, but that ongoing salvation required the believer to cooperate with grace through good works, penance, indulgences, and participation in the sacraments. This was encapsulated in the concept of *fides formata*—faith formed by love. Faith on its own was considered insufficient unless enlivened by ritualistic deeds.

Despite Luther's rigorous monastic discipline, he struggled to find peace with God. He later wrote, "I hated that word 'righteousness of God,' which according to the use and custom of all the teachers, I had been taught to understand philosophically . . . as the formal or active righteousness as they called it, with which God is righteous and punishes the unrighteous sinner."[1] Luther's theological breakthrough came through his reading of Rom 1:17 where Paul states, "For in it the righteousness of God is revealed from faith for faith, as it is written, 'The righteous shall live by faith.'" Luther came to understand that the "righteousness of God" is not an attribute by which God judges but a gift that God gives to the believer. Luther later wrote, "Here I felt that I was altogether born again and had entered paradise itself through open gates."[2]

From this exegetical insight emerged the doctrine of justification by faith alone (*sola fide*), which is inseparable from *sola gratia* ("grace alone"). Luther argued that grace is the foundation of salvation, and faith is the instrument by which it is received. For Luther, this grace is unmerited and monergistic. Thus, God alone acts to justify the sinner. Luther writes in his Heidelberg Disputation, "The love of God does not find, but creates, that which is pleasing to it."[3] This departure from the medieval notion of *gratia infusa* ("infused grace") redefined grace as God's favorable disposition toward sinners. It was a relational and declarative act. The sinner is justified *extra nos* ("outside of oneself") by the righteousness of Christ imputed, not imparted.

Luther's doctrine of grace is grounded in his *theologia crucis* ("theology of the cross"). In contrast to a "theology of glory," which sees human progress and moral achievement as a path to God, the theology of the cross insists that God is most fully revealed in suffering and apparent defeat. Grace, then, is a divine intervention to rescue the helpless. In the Heidelberg Disputation, Luther states, "He deserves to be called a theologian . . . who comprehends the visible and manifest things of God seen through suffering

---

1. Luther, *Preface*, 336–37.
2. Luther, *Preface*, 337.
3. Luther, Heidelberg Disputation, Thesis 28.

and the cross."[4] The cross becomes the hermeneutical key to understanding divine grace. It is a gift mediated through the crucified Christ.

Though Luther rejected the Roman Catholic sacramental system as a mechanism of merit, he did not abandon the sacraments altogether. Rather, he redefined them as means by which God conveys his promises. In the *Small Catechism*, Luther taught that baptism "signifies that the old creature in us with all sins and evil desires is to be drowned and die through daily contrition and repentance."[5] However, he maintained that faith receives these gifts. Likewise, for Luther, the Lord's Supper is a real participation in the body and blood of Christ. Scripture is the vehicle by which grace is made effective. Luther writes in *On the Freedom of a Christian*, "Faith clings to the Word and trusts it."[6] Luther's paradoxical dictum from *The Freedom of a Christian* illustrates this point: "A Christian is a perfectly free lord of all, subject to none. A Christian is a perfectly dutiful servant of all, subject to all."[7] Grace liberates from self-justification, which in turn opens the door to genuine love.

Despite its theological power, Luther's doctrine of grace has drawn criticism. Roman Catholic scholars argue that it diminishes sanctification by isolating justification from moral transformation. Grace, in this critique, becomes forensic but not formative. Furthermore, later Protestant traditions influenced by Luther—especially some strands of Lutheranism and evangelicalism—have sometimes been charged with promoting a kind of "cheap grace," to borrow Dietrich Bonhoeffer's phrase, where race is preached without discipleship, forgiveness without repentance, justification without sanctification.[8] To that end, grace must be understood as foundational but in conjunction with obedient faith.

IS THERE A BALANCE?

Biblically, neither works-based salvation nor *sola fide* can be true by itself. As James writes, "Even the demons believe and shudder!" (Jas 2:19). Faith is only expressed in obedience and grace is not earned by works. Peter preached, "Repent and be baptized every one of you in the name of Jesus

---

4. Luther, Heidelberg Disputation, Thesis 20.
5. Luther, *Small Catechism*, 232.
6. Luther, *Freedom of a Christian*, in Grimm, *Luther's Works* 31:345.
7. Luther, *Freedom of a Christian*, in Grimm, *Luther's Works* 31:344.
8. Bonhoeffer, *Cost of Discipleship*, 45.

Christ for the forgiveness of your sins" (Acts 2:38). Baptism, in this view, is not a work of merit but a faith response to the grace of God offered in Jesus Christ. As Jack Cottrell notes, "Faith and baptism are the means of grace, not its source. They are conditions of salvation, not causes."[9] This harmonizes well passages like Eph 2:8–9 with texts like Jas 2:24. In fact, after stating that those in Christ are saved by grace through faith in Eph 2:8, Paul writes in Eph 2:10, "For we are his workmanship, created in Christ Jesus for good works, which God prepared beforehand, that we should walk in them." Christians are new creations in Christ. This new creation has a purpose—good works. Thus, Christians do good works because salvation does not and cannot come through works of merit.

CONCLUSION

Martin Luther's doctrine of grace—*sola gratia*—stands as a theological recovery in the history of Christian thought. By proclaiming that salvation is by grace alone through faith alone, Luther refocused Christianity on the gospel of divine mercy. His teaching continues to inspire theologians and lay Christians to the present day. Yet, Luther's formulation, though noble and necessary, requires supplementation. Grace must be received through obedient faith expressed in baptism, and it must lead to a life of holiness empowered by the Spirit. The tension between divine grace and human response is not a contradiction but a covenantal harmony. As Paul writes in Phil 2:12–13, "Work out your own salvation with fear and trembling, for it is God who works in you." Salvation is certainly by grace. The difference lies not in the source but in the shape of the response.

---

9. Cottrell, *Faith Once for All*, 289.

16

The Doctrines of Election and Predestination

AMONG THE MOST CONTROVERSIAL theological tenets in Christian history is the doctrine of election. Rooted in the writings of Augustine and systematized by John Calvin in the sixteenth century, the doctrine posits that God, from eternity, has unconditionally elected some to salvation and others to damnation. While proponents argue this view upholds God's sovereignty, critics claim it undermines the reality of free will (a necessary aspect of God's love) and contradicts the offer of salvation to "whosoever will" found in Scripture (cf. John 3:16). This chapter will examine the biblical, theological, and historical underpinnings of the doctrine of unconditional election, then offer an analysis arguing the insufficiency of this doctrine.

HISTORICAL ROOTS OF CALVINISTIC ELECTION

The Calvinistic doctrine of election finds its roots in the theology of Augustine of Hippo (AD 354–430), who, in response to Pelagius, emphasized the utter depravity of man and the necessity of divine grace for salvation. Augustine articulated a view of predestination in which God elects individuals to salvation unconditionally and irresistibly.[1] John Calvin (1509–64) refined this

---

1. See McGrath, *Christian Theology*, 420–23.

The Doctrines of Election and Predestination

concept in his *Institutes of the Christian Religion*, where he defined election as "the eternal decree of God, by which he has determined in himself what he would have to become of every individual of mankind."[2] Calvin argued that this election is based solely on the mysterious will of God.

The Synod of Dort (1618–19), in response to the Remonstrant movement led by Jacobus Arminius, codified the Calvinistic understanding of salvation in the five points commonly remembered by the acronym TULIP:

1. Total Depravity—Humans are utterly incapable of choosing God without divine intervention.

2. Unconditional Election—God's choice of the elect is not based on any foreseen virtue or faith.

3. Limited Atonement—Christ died only for the elect.

4. Irresistible Grace—The elect cannot resist God's calling.

5. Perseverance of the Saints—The elect will persevere to the end and thus the truly elect cannot lose their salvation.

Election, therefore, is theological center of the Calvinistic system.

Calvinists often point to a series of key texts to support the doctrine. Romans 9 is perhaps the central prooftext where Paul writes, "Though they were not yet born and had done nothing either good or bad—in order that God's purpose of election might continue, not because of works but because of him who calls" (Rom 9:11). Calvinists argue that this indicates God's sovereign choice apart from human will. The analogy of the potter and clay in Rom 9:21 is further cited to emphasize the divine prerogative. Another foundational passage is Eph 1:3–11 where Paul writes that believers were "chosen in him before the foundation of the world" (Eph 1:4).

Jesus's teachings in John 6 at face value seem to support this perspective as Jesus declares, "All that the Father gives me will come to me," and "No one can come to me unless the Father who sent me draws him" (John 6:37, 44). Calvinists interpret these verses as evidence of both divine initiative and the irresistibility of grace, though many often ignore John 6:45, which states, "Everyone who has heard and learned from the Father comes to me." This further reading in the same context implies (1) willful hearing and (2) action on behalf of the believer, something Calvinists deny.

---

2. Calvin, *Institutes* 3.21.5.

Section Two

THEOLOGICAL IMPLICATIONS OF CALVINISTIC ELECTION

The doctrine of election emphasizes the sovereignty of God. Therefore, the elect are secure because God's decrees are immutable. However, this leads to the more controversial doctrine of double predestination. This view suggests that God not only elects some to salvation but actively decrees others to damnation. Though logically consistent within the Calvinistic framework, this view has drawn significant criticism. Critics argue that it presents a deterministic portrait of God that undermines human responsibility and portrays divine justice as arbitrary. Proponents, however, maintain that double predestination upholds the biblical witness to God's ultimate authority over all things, including salvation and judgment.

This emphasis on divine initiative often diminishes or dismisses the role of the church in evangelism and mission. If God has eternally and unchangeably decreed both the salvation of the elect and the damnation of the reprobate, the necessity or efficacy of evangelistic activity is unnecessary. Thus, evangelism would be incapable of altering the divinely determined destinies of individuals. Such a framework risks promoting fatalism, wherein evangelism becomes a formality rather than a genuine appeal to all. Moreover, the universal language of the Great Commission (Matt 28:18–20) and Paul's insistence that "faith comes from hearing" (Rom 10:17) suggest that the preaching of the gospel plays an essential and instrumental role in God's salvific economy. Thus, while proponents of double predestination often defend evangelism as the ordained means through which God calls the elect (who by the standards of presentation are already elect regardless of being called via evangelism), the doctrine may nevertheless introduce practical and theological tensions regarding the scope, urgency, and sincerity of gospel proclamation.

A FREE-WILL PERSPECTIVE

Can there be a theology in which grace and human freedom coexist? Can God remain sovereign while also providing no control over the will of humans? How far does God's sovereignty extend? Texts such as 1 Tim 2:3–4 and 2 Pet 3:9 are key. In 1 Tim 2:4, Paul writes that God "desires all people to be saved and come to the knowledge of the truth," and Peter affirms in 2 Pet 3:9 that God is "not wishing that any should perish, but that all should reach repentance." Additionally, the golden text of Scripture, John 3:16, states that "whosoever believes should not perish." Both passages use the Greek term *pas* ("all"), which demands a view of the whole. These affirmations challenge the idea that God has elected only a select few for salvation.

Jesus's lament over Jerusalem in Matt 23:37 offers another compelling counterpoint. He says, "O Jerusalem, Jerusalem, the city that kills the prophets and stones those who are sent to it! How often would I have gathered your children together as a hen gathers her brood under her wings, *and you were not willing!*" (emphasis added). This verse indicates that divine will can be resisted and that humans bear responsibility for their response to God. Even Rom 9, which is frequently cited by Calvinists, does not support individual predestination. In Rom 9, Paul addresses corporate election—i.e., the roles of Israel and the gentiles in God's redemptive history. Thus, the broader context of Rom 9–11 suggests a more inclusive understanding of God's plan. This inclusive framework is strengthened by Paul's argument in Rom 10 where faith comes by hearing and hearing by the word of Christ (Rom 10:17). Paul's proclamation presupposes a human response. Paul does not treat salvation as a divine imposition but as a call that must be heard, believed, and obeyed.

The doctrine of unconditional election raises serious concerns about divine justice and human accountability. If God unconditionally elects some to salvation and others to damnation, on what basis are the non-elect condemned? Additionally, the Calvinist view challenges the biblical portrayal of God's love for all who are created in his image. Again, John 3:16 states, "God so loved the world," not only the elect. If God withholds saving grace from some, can his love truly be universal? Further, can humans be held responsible for failing to believe in a gospel they were never given the grace to accept?

The fact is that Scripture teaches that the gospel of Jesus Christ is universally available to "whosoever believes." The elect mentioned in Eph 1 and elsewhere refers to the church, not to the individual. Thus, God had always known that those who are in the body of Christ would be saved while those who are not would be condemned. This places the emphasis on the group rather than on the individual. The individual must choose to be chosen. Grace is offered freely, but it must be received through faith and obedience.

Section Two

PREDESTINATION

Within the Calvinist tradition, the doctrine of predestination—whereby God from eternity freely and unchangeably ordains all whom he will save—functions as a doctrinal keystone linking the attributes of divine sovereignty, providence, and grace.[3] Yet both within and beyond the Reformation heritage, rival construals such as classical Arminianism, Molinism, Barthian "Christological election," and various libertarian proposals have persistently challenged Calvinist claims.

Although John Calvin's name has become virtually synonymous with predestination, the concept's pedigree predates the Reformation. Augustine of Hippo, writing against Pelagius, grounded salvation wholly in divine elective mercy. Augustine wrote, "For not all are called according to purpose, but those who are elected are those who are called according to purpose" (Augustine, *De Dono Perseverantiae* 16). Augustine thus forged the soteriological grammar—grace as unmerited, effectual, and particular—that would later inform Protestant formulations.

Calvin systematized Augustine's insights within a comprehensive theology of *sola gratia*. In *Institutes* 3.21–24, he distinguished between *election* unto life and *reprobation* unto destruction.[4] While contemporaries such as Martin Bucer and Heinrich Bullinger affirmed unconditional election, Calvin's dialectical precision—*praedestinatio* as "the eternal decree of God, by which he has determined with himself what he would have to become of every individual" (3.21.5)—became the hallmark of what later critics labeled "Calvinism." Classical Reformed confessions such as the Second Helvetic Confession (1562) and the Westminster Confession of Faith (1646) echoed the Synod of Dordt in asserting unconditional election while refusing to make God the "author of sin."

PROOFTEXTS FOR PREDESTINATION

Calvinists argue that predestination motifs pervade Israel's Scriptures. Deuteronomy frames Israel's identity in the sovereign affection of Yahweh (e.g., Deut 7:7–8). Prophetic literature extends election to the Servant figure whose redemptive mission encompasses the nations (Isa 42:1–9). Romans 8:28–30 delineates an unbroken "chain"

---

3. Calvin, *Institutes* 3.21.5.
4. Calvin, *Institutes* 3.23.1.

The Doctrines of Election and Predestination

(foreknowledge-predestination-calling-justification-glorification) that grounds believers' assurance in God's invincible purpose. Romans 9 intensifies the theme through the twin illustrations of Isaac/Ishmael and Jacob/Esau by climaxing in the potter-clay metaphor of Rom 9:20–23. Ephesians 1:3–14 further portrays election as "in Christ . . . before the foundation of the world," which seems to link predestination to adoption (vv. 5–6, 12). This Christocentric framing has been pivotal for Reformed theologians who, following Calvin's *unio cum Christo*, insist that election is a firm decision made by God.

The Fourth Gospel's appeal to divine initiative—"No one can come to me unless the Father who sent me draws him" (John 6:44)—reinforces a monergistic soteriology. Calvinist interpreters read the verb *helkō* ("to draw") as effectual attraction, whereas Arminian exegesis construes it as "enablement" that may be resisted.[5] The text's relational context ("all that the Father gives me will come") suggests a divine gift that secures its telos.

THEOLOGICAL RATIONALE FOR CALVINISTIC PREDESTINATION

The doctrine of Calvinistic predestination arises from the axiomatic conviction that God is the "first cause" who "works all things according to the counsel of his will" (Eph 1:11). The doctrine thus embodies a theocentric teleology, namely that redemption magnifies divine glory precisely because salvation from inception to consummation is of grace alone.[6] The Pauline description of spiritual death in Eph 2:1–3 undergirds the Reformed claim that saving faith is the fruit of regenerative grace (Eph 2:8–9). Thus, unconditional election coheres with effectual calling wherein the Spirit irresistibly vivifies the elect—a position commonly described as "monergism."

Calvinists contend that if God is simple and immutable, his knowledge cannot be conditioned by one's self-determinations. In contrast, Molinists posit middle knowledge (*scientia media*), whereby God contingently grounds future contingents through logically prior foreknowledge of permissive choices.

---

5. Warfield, "Predestination," 283–88; Bavinck, *Sin and Salvation*, 38–40.
6. Bavinck, *Sin and Salvation*, 38–40.

Section Two

ALTERNATIVE VIEWS

Jacobus Arminius (1560–1609) affirmed that grace enables but does not necessitate faith, thereby conditioning election on God's foreknowledge of those who freely believe.[7] Contemporary Arminians argue that this preserves God's universal salvific will (cf. 1 Tim 2:4). Calvinists counter suggesting that foreseen-faith election subordinates divine causality to creaturely contingencies and collapses grace in favor of merit.[8] Moreover, if total depravity precludes autonomous turning, prevenient grace must itself be discriminating, effectively reintroducing unconditional election under a different label.

Open theists argue that genuine relationality requires God to forgo exhaustive definite foreknowledge of the future. Calvinists regard this as a radical revision of classical theism that jeopardizes prophetic certainty and the sovereignty of God. Karl Barth famously "relocated" election in the person of Jesus Christ when he suggested that God elects himself for humanity and humanity in himself.[9] While some Calvinists applaud Barth for intensifying the incarnational center, critics note that a universal election "in Christ" risks dissolving the qualitative distinction between elect and reprobate, thereby obscuring warnings of judgment.[10]

The most fundamental objection to Calvinistic predestination is that it contradicts the express desire of God that all people be saved. The Bible clearly uses the language of "predestination" (e.g., Rom 8:29–30; Eph 1:4–5), but these passages must be interpreted in their contexts. In Eph 1, Paul discusses the corporate election of those who are "in Christ." God predestined that salvation would be found *in Christ* and those who freely respond in faith and obedience are added to that elect body (cf. Acts 2:47; Gal 3:26–27). The emphasis is on God choosing a plan and a people in and through his Son, Jesus Christ.

God has endowed humanity with the ability to accept or reject his invitation. Jesus repeatedly called people to "come" (cf. Matt 11:28), and the book of Acts is filled with appeals to repent, believe, and be baptized (Acts 2:38; 3:19; 8:36–38; 22:16). The gospel invitation is genuinely open to all, and God holds each person responsible for their decision

---

7. Arminius, *Works of Jacobus Arminius*, 659–61.
8. Horton, *Christian Faith*, 318–22.
9. Barth, *Doctrine of God*, 94–104.
10. McCormack, *Karl Barth's Theology*, 92–97.

(cf. 2 Cor 5:10). To say otherwise is to make God the author of sin. If people are predestined to salvation or damnation irrespective of their will, then divine judgment appears arbitrary and unjust, which would contradict God's character (cf. Gen 18:25).

The predestinarian framework often requires one to reinterpret or minimize many plain passages of Scripture to preserve systematic consistency. In contrast, believers must speak where the Bible speaks how the Bible speaks. The doctrine of predestination, as commonly framed, violates this principle by elevating a theological construct over the clear gospel message of those who heard, believed, and obeyed.

CONCLUSION

The Calvinistic doctrines of election and predestination seek to offer an explanation of God's sovereignty, humanity's depravity, and the Christian's security. However, a synergistic view in which God's grace and human free will work together offers a more balanced interpretation. It preserves divine initiative without negating human responsibility. While the issue of divine election will continue to be the subject of much theological debate, it is vital that any formulation of the doctrine uphold both God's sovereignty and humanity's responsibility and accountability. As Rev 22:17 affirms, "The Spirit and the Bride say, 'Come.' And let the one who hears say, 'Come.' And let the one who is thirsty come; let the one who desires take the water of life without price."

17

Once Saved, Always Saved?

IT IS HARD TO imagine a question more capable of unsettling an earnest Christian than the possibility of falling from grace. In classical Calvinism the question is settled with a confident negative: God's elect can neither totally nor finally lose salvation. Popularly summarized as "once saved, always saved," the doctrine of the perseverance of the saints (*perseverantia sanctorum*) flows from the same sovereign grace that first awakens faith. This doctrine has sustained the assurance of Reformed believers for nearly five centuries.[1] What follows weaves together the doctrine's historical development and systematic coherence, after which an alternative reading of Scripture and tradition is offered that challenges this claim.

John Calvin did not invent the English slogan, but his *Institutes* leave no doubt that enduring faith is guaranteed by God's unchangeable decree. He writes, "God has chosen us out of his own good pleasure, and not according to our own merit. For before we were born we had done neither good nor evil. God therefore was moved by nothing but his own mercy."[2] Election rests on the *immutabile decretum*, that is, the regenerated must reach glory because the will of the triune God cannot be thwarted. When the Arminian Remonstrants questioned this logic, the Synod of Dort (1619) answered with its Fifth Head of Doctrine: the regenerate are

---

1. Berkhof, *Systematic Theology*, 546–53.
2. Calvin, *Institutes* 3.24.6–8.

"certainly kept by God . . . and can never fall totally nor finally from the state of grace."[3] That article completed the famed TULIP (total depravity, unconditional election, limited atonement, irresistible grace, and perseverance of the saints) theology by giving perseverance its place as the capstone. Post-Reformation scholars such as Francis Turretin distinguished between temporary and saving faith, thereby explaining why some church members lapse while the elect persevere.[4] In the nineteenth century, Princeton theologian B. B. Warfield framed the same conviction as the indispensable foundation for Christian assurance. He argued, should perseverance fail, the entire redemptive plan would be hostage to human faithlessness.[5] Thus, God's faithful character guarantees the believer's final glory because God began it of his own will and election.

Calvinists argue that Jesus promised his sheep shall "never perish" and that "no one will snatch them" from his hand or the Father's (John 10:28–29). Paul further seems to argue that nothing "in all creation" can separate believers from God's love (Rom 8:39). The Epistle to the Hebrews adds a priestly dimension by asserting that Christ "is able to save completely those who draw near to God through him, since he always lives to make intercession" (Heb 7:25). Pauline theology further describes believers as "sealed" by the Spirit "for the day of redemption" (Eph 4:30), which seems to indicate irreversible and total ownership. In each case, the Calvinistic reading sees a unilateral divine initiative whose efficacy cannot be compromised.

On systematic grounds perseverance argues that adoption is irrevocable, Christ's intercession cannot fail, and the Spirit's indwelling guarantees glorification. The Westminster Confession (17.1–3) balances this promise with sober warnings, namely that true believers may fall into grievous sin, but God's covenant love will restore them through discipline and will never relinquish the soul for whom Christ died. Thus, this assurance is offered on the objective character of God. Far from encouraging moral laxity, say its defenders, confidence of final salvation liberates believers for obedience motivated by gratitude rather than fear. Indeed, the traditional Reformed maxim insists that perseverance is inseparable from holiness. If a professing Christian shows no fruit of the Christian walk, the most likely diagnosis is counterfeit faith rather than the loss of genuine salvation. Thus, the

---

3. Synod of Dort, *Canons*, Fifth Head, art. 3–4, in Schaff, *Creeds of Christendom* 3:521–22.

4. Turretin, *Institutes of Elenctic Theology* 2:587–613.

5. Warfield, "On the Biblical Notion," 351.

Calvinist would argue that a true conversion never occurred. Therefore, one cannot "fall from salvation" if that one never *truly* had salvation at all.

A REBUTTAL

Yet the same canon of Scripture contains texts that many theologians read as describing a real, not hypothetical, apostasy. Hebrews 6:4–6 speaks of those "once enlightened," who have "tasted the heavenly gift" and been made "partakers of the Holy Spirit," yet who have "fallen away." If such phrases cannot apply to authentic believers, critics argue, the rhetoric loses its gravity. Second Peter 2:20–22 portrays people who have "escaped the defilements of the world through the knowledge of the Lord and Savior Jesus Christ" only to become re-entangled, their last state worse than the first. Further, Paul warns gentile Christians that if they do not "continue in [God's] kindness" they too "will be cut off" (Rom 11:22). Jesus's vine metaphor in John 15 likewise envisions branches that are "in me" but ultimately wither and are burned because they do not remain in him, implying they have departed, dried up, and are not bearing fruit (John 15:1–6).

Historically, the notion that salvation can be forfeited is hardly a theological novelty. Irenaeus, Tertullian, and John Chrysostom all assumed that post-baptismal sin could destroy the life of grace. Augustine, though he spoke eloquently of predestining grace, still permitted the possibility that a person regenerated in water and Spirit could fall from salvation through persistent sin.[6] That position remains the majority view of Eastern Orthodoxy, Roman Catholicism, and large swaths of Protestantism.

Covenant relationships necessitate activity on behalf of both parties. To be sure, God initiated the relationship from the foundation of the world and formalized the relationship in the new covenant of Christ, but humans must receive and cooperate with God's grace. New Testament verbs like "continue," "hold fast," and "work out" presume that the believer's ongoing response is neither automatic nor coerced (cf. Phil 2:12; Col 1:23; Heb 3:14). Subsequently, Jesus's sheep are identified as the ones who continued listening to his voice. These warnings demonstrate that the relationship can be ruptured if one's genuine faith turns to unbelief.

What then of Calvinism's exegetical linchpins? Romans 8 and John 10, read in context, contain implicit conditions. Paul's promise is addressed to Christians. A subsequent life of unbelief would remove a person from the

---

6. See Picirilli, *Grace, Faith, Free Will*, 147–64.

promise's scope. The fault is not God's but the one who left the faith. Jesus's assurance in John 10:27 is directed to sheep who are listening (*akouousin*; present participle indicating an ongoing action). Nothing external can snatch them, but the text does not deny that a sheep might cease to heed the Shepherd's voice. Likewise, the Spirit's "seal" language in Eph 1 need not entail irreversible safety. A seal can be broken. Moreover, the book of Hebrews balances high-Christological confidence with uncompromising warnings precisely because its author believes real apostasy is possible and is presently happening in the churches to whom he writes.

CONCLUSION

The doctrine of the perseverance of the saints ("once saved, always saved") offers bracing assurance that God's purpose cannot fail. The alternative view insists that covenantal love is relational and therefore resistible. Love must be freely given and freely received. If it is not, it cannot be sincere love. Either the one who offers the love does so out of obligation or the one who receives the love accepts it out of compulsion. Nonetheless, both sides agree that God is faithful, that Christ's atonement is sufficient, and that the Spirit empowers Christian endurance. However, they differ over whether grace works irresistibly or cooperatively. The end of the matter is that salvation's security is not found in an abstract syllogism but in a living faith that abides in the crucified and risen Lord Jesus Christ. To be sure, if one is saved, one must behave in accordance with the will of God and standard of Christ.

18

Calvin and the Purpose of Prayer

PRAYER STANDS AT THE crossroads of theology and devotion. No Reformer probed that intersection more thoroughly than John Calvin, who said that prayer is "a perpetual exercise of faith" (*Institutes* 3.20). Yet, twentieth and twenty-first century theologians have queried whether Calvin's logic fully captures the open, raw, and dialogical energy of prayer. Randall Bailey in his 2021 book *Improving Your Prayer Life Through a Study of the Psalter* presses that critique by urging today's worshipers to recover the audacity, bargaining, and emotional openness found in the psalms.[1] This chapter first synthesizes Calvin's stated reasons for prayer, then measures them against the approach to prayer found specifically in the psalms.

CALVIN'S SIXFOLD LOGIC FOR PRAYER

If God already knows, why ask? Calvin anticipates this chief objection and answers with a six-part rationale.

> It is therefore by the benefit of prayer that we reach those riches which are laid up for us with the heavenly Father. For there is a kind of intercourse between God and men, by which, having entered the heavenly sanctuary, they appeal to him in person concerning his promises, that when necessity requires, they may learn

---

1. See Bailey, *Improving Your Prayer Life*, 1–17.

> by experience that what they believed simply on the basis of the word was not in vain. First, reverence to God, and to be of such mind as befits those who enter into converse with God. Second, a sense of want, and a feeling of our own poverty to drive and spur us to seek God. Third, to yield all confidence in ourselves and humbly plead for pardon. Fourth, to be so assured of the event, as that we doubt not but that our prayers shall be heard. Unless we are supported by his intercession, there is no access for us to the Father's throne. For as soon as God's majesty comes to mind, we cannot but tremble . . . until Christ comes forward to calm our fears, and to lead us to hope and to trust in him, and to rest in the confidence of being heard through him.[2]

Thus, God commands prayer (1) to bring about more desire for him, (2) to purge immoral thoughts by placing them in divine light, (3) to prepare a grateful heart, (4) to deepen our awareness of providence, (5) to make us active participants in God's work, and (6) to confirm faith experientially as we trace answered petitions back to God as the source. For Calvin, then, prayer is less about informing an omniscient God and more about reforming an oblivious human to God's already set will.

Calvin supplements his rationale with four "rules." The first is reverence. The petitioner must approach in awe with a mind willing to engage and a heart that is alert. The second is poverty of spirit, which leads to the third, humility. Pride must be silenced. The fourth is confidence. Prayers should be asked in assurance that the Father hears his people. These rules support the Genevan liturgy, which placed a long congregational confession before intercession and cherished the Lord's Prayer as a paradigm for balanced petitions.

THE PSALMISTS' COUNTERPROPOSAL

Calvin loved the psalms—publishing five editions of his commentary on the book—yet he studied them primarily for Christological and instructive patterns. He seldom lingered over their boldness in asking God to change his mind or fix a situation seemingly contrary to his will. By reading the imprecatory psalms as typological of Christ's zeal for justice and the lament psalms as a prophecy of the crucifixion, Calvin channeled the psalmists' emotive force but neglects to allow for God's mind to change or for God to be prompted to intervene in a moment in which God was not originally planning to intervene.

2. Calvin, *Institutes* 3.20.3–5

Randall Bailey revisits those same texts with different questions. Noting how often the psalmists "bargain" with God (e.g., Ps 22:22), Bailey contends that biblical prayer is interactive and transactional. The petitioner reminds God of his covenant obligations, expects a concrete response, and promises public praise in return. Prayer then becomes a reciprocal process whereby humans may bring pressures on God. For example, this tension is particularly evident in the narrative of Moses's intercession in Exod 33. Following Israel's idolatry with the golden calf, Moses appeals to God not to abandon his people. In a striking response, the Lord replies, "I will do the very thing you have asked, because I am pleased with you and I know you by name" (Exod 33:17). The text portrays a genuine dialogical exchange in which Moses's plea directly impacts God's response. This episode suggests that intercessory prayer functions within a relational framework where God, though sovereign, is responsive. The implication is that God allows for contingency within the divine-human relationship.

A similar challenge to Calvinistic determinism arises in the account of Hannah's prayer in 1 Sam 1. Deeply distressed by her barrenness, Hannah pours out her soul before the Lord, vowing that if he grants her a son, she will dedicate the child to God (1 Sam 1:11). The narrative presents her petition as raw, heartfelt, and specific. The Lord's response—"and the Lord remembered her" (1 Sam 1:19)—is framed as a direct answer. The text emphasizes God's compassion and his responsiveness to our petition. Within a Calvinistic framework that views all events as unalterably foreordained, Hannah's desperate plea and the Lord's gracious response are theologically incompatible and offers a hollow reading of the text. Yet, the biblical witness suggests that God has chosen to act in ways that take human agency into account.

Calvin's first reason for prayer—to ignite godly desire—risks reducing prayer to therapy. The psalmists, by contrast, often voice their desires unfiltered. David does not sanitize his frustration when he asks, "How long, O Lord? Will you forget me forever?" (Ps 13:1). Calvin's second motive—exposing unworthy desires—assumes a linear maturation: speak desire, recognize its folly, repent. Yet, the searing imprecation of Ps 137:9—"Blessed shall he be who takes your little ones and dashes them against the rock!"—sits unrepented within Scripture. Rather than purging the emotion, the canon preserves it, forcing the praying community to wrestle with vengeance, grief, and justice. Leaving such prayers intact teaches the legitimacy of lament, which is a form of prayer seldom encouraged in Calvinist liturgies.

Calvin's third and fourth points—gratitude for gifts and confirmation of providence—ring true to the Psalter, but the directional flow differs. Calvin imagines gift first, gratitude second; the psalmists often invert the order by pledging gratitude in advance as leverage for deliverance (e.g., Ps 30:12). Such "vow-praise" structures show that biblical petition can be conditional. For example, in Ps 30, the psalmist asks God for healing. If healing does not come, the psalmist states he will not be around to worship. The bargaining honors God's character by acknowledging that God is able to fulfill the request and appeals to God's desire for praise among his people.

Calvin's fifth and sixth motives treat unanswered prayers as pedagogical. God often gives the impression of sleeping to rouse lethargic saints; yet, many psalms insist the silence itself is the crisis, not the remedy. Note the psalmist's words in Ps 44:23, "Why are you sleeping, Lord? Awake!," where the psalmist gives space for lament and accusation. Where Calvin calls believers to examine themselves when God delays, the psalmists instead critique God because he delays. They prove confident enough in their relationship with God to question his timing.

A deeper disagreement concerns the effectiveness of prayer. Calvin emphatically denies that prayer changes God's will; instead, it is the ordained means by which God executes what he has already willed—a secondary causality nested in providence. However, many psalms assume real contingency. God relented of intended judgment when Moses interceded (Ps 106:23), and Hezekiah's life was lengthened through prayer (Ps 116:1–4 echoing 2 Kgs 20). The requests of the petitioner changed the outcome through God's grace and mercy. Nowhere is the relational depth of prayer more evident than in Jesus's plea in Gethsemane: "Father, if you are willing, remove this cup from me. Nevertheless, not my will, but yours, be done" (Luke 22:42). Jesus's words here reflect a genuine desire for an alternative to the suffering that lay ahead. His request is a real petition that seeks, if possible, a different path. In doing so, the incarnate Son asks the Father to reconsider the necessity of the cross—a moment that clearly depicts a sincere effort to change the course of action. Importantly, this expression is not sinful, nor does it imply faithlessness. Rather, it affirms the legitimacy of petitioning God even in moments where his will may ultimately remain firm. Jesus's prayer in the garden reveals that wrestling with God in prayer is not only permitted but sanctified in the life of faith. The sinless Christ models the kind of honest engagement with God that Calvinism too easily dismisses.

CONCLUSION

John Calvin portrays prayer as the God-ordained means by which believers' wills are bent toward God's divine purpose. The psalms, however, paint prayer as a gritty, reciprocal engagement capable of wrestling, bargaining, and mourning in God's presence. Given the biblical witnesses, we again must ask the following questions as the issue of prayer rests on God's foreknowledge. If God knows everything, then why do we pray at all? Won't things just happen because God controls everything? If my salvation was foreordained, and I cannot refuse it, why do we evangelize? If I cannot lose my salvation, why do I need to follow the commandments? These questions demonstrate the absurdity of Calvin's doctrines. Scripture depicts the Christian in relationship with the divine. Prayer then is communication of the best kind.

19

Calvinism and Baptism

CHRISTIAN HISTORY BRIMS WITH debate over baptism. Nowhere is the disagreement sharper than between the Reformed tradition and movements that insist the rite is essential for salvation. Calvin extolled baptism as a "sealed instrument" of grace, yet he stopped short of locating regeneration in the water itself. Later Reformed confessions followed his logic by treating baptism as a covenantal pledge whose absence can be overcome by the Spirit. Opponents reply that Scripture binds forgiveness, union with Christ, and the new birth to the very moment of immersion in baptism and that the earliest believers read the texts exactly that way. What follows traces Calvin's theology of baptism then offers a rebuttal that contends for the rite's essential role in the ordinary economy of salvation.

CALVIN'S THEOLOGY OF BAPTISM

Calvin's most concentrated teaching on baptism appears in *Institutes* 4.15–16. Calvin argued that the water "has no virtue in itself." Thus, its power derives wholly from the Spirit who applies Christ's benefits as he wills (*Institutes* 4.15.14). Calvin extended baptism to infants invoking the analogy of circumcision as the covenant's earlier sign (*Institutes* 4.16.6–10). Crucially, Calvin separates the moment of regeneration from the moment of baptism. Calvin argued that to tether new birth inseparably to the sacrament would make salvation contingent on human administration and would restrain God's sovereignty over salvation. Yet, Calvin did not reduce baptism to a symbol as many Reformed theologians do today. In Calvin's church order, the sacrament also functions ecclesiologically. In other words, Calvin argued that baptism does not add one to the body of Christ but does serve as initiation into the congregation (*Institutes* 4.15.1).

The Heidelberg Catechism (1563) celebrates baptism as the pledge "that Christ's blood and [the] Spirit wash us from all sins," while immediately clarifying that "merely the outward washing" accomplishes nothing apart from faith.[1] The Westminster Confession of Faith (1646) devotes two chapters (27–28) to sacramental theology and calls baptism a "sign and seal of the covenant of grace . . . of remission of sins," yet insists that "grace and salvation are not so inseparably annexed . . . that no person can be regenerated or saved without it" (27.1, 28.5). Both documents preserve Calvin's insistence that the sacrament confers what it signifies—remission, cleansing, adoption but only to those whom the Spirit has already inwardly renewed.

A CASE FOR BAPTISM'S NECESSITY

Set against Calvin's view of baptism as a sign of already present faith and as inauguration into a congregation stands another view that reads the New Testament and early patristic witness more literally. Four lines of argument converge: the apostolic kerygma, the practice of the primitive church, the logic of union with Christ, and the consistency of Christian initiation.

The earliest sermons of the New Testament church (specifically recorded in the book of Acts) bind baptism with the forgiveness of sins. On Pentecost Peter answers a convicted crowd with the command, "Repent and be baptized every one of you for the forgiveness of your sins and you will receive the gift of the Holy Spirit" (Acts 2:38). After meeting Jesus on the road to Damascus, an anxious Saul asks the Christian Ananias what he must do, to which Ananias responds, "Rise and be baptized, and wash away your sins" (Acts 22:16), just as Peter told the Jews in Jerusalem. Peter later wrote in his first letter, "Baptism now saves you, not as a removal of dirt from the body but as an appeal to God for a good conscience, through the resurrection of Jesus Christ" (1 Pet 3:21). Paul situates participation in Christ's death, burial, and resurrection within baptism (cf. Rom 6:3–4; Col 2:12). As such, Paul proclaims, "As many of you as were baptized into

---

1. *Heidelberg Catechism*, "Lord's Days" 26–27, in Leith, *Confessions*, 64–66.

Christ have put on Christ" (Gal 3:27). Contrary to Calvin's view, these texts describe the rite as how one receives salvation and justification in Christ.

EARLY CHURCH CONSENSUS

Second-century writers agree that baptism is essential for salvation, though disagreement exists concerning the manner and means by which baptism should occur. Justin Martyr calls baptism "the bath of regeneration," received for "remission of sins formerly committed" (Justin Martyr, *First Apology* 61). Everett Ferguson's exhaustive survey concludes that until Augustine no major writer denies baptism's saving efficacy.[2] Even Augustine never detached regeneration from baptism.

The hermeneutic of baptism shared by the church fathers of the second century is twofold. First, there is a hermeneutic of divine institution. Each source assumes God instituted baptism from the point of creation by linking the Spirit mentioned in John 3:5 with the Spirit that hovers over the waters in Gen 1:2. Thus, for these theologians, God intended for baptism to be essential from the beginning, even presenting baptism to the Jews in the form of the Red Sea crossing and ceremonial washings of the Levitical system. Second, there is a hermeneutic of community. Whereas baptism in the New Testament is often done privately (perhaps within the context of a family like that of Cornelius or the Philippian jailer), baptism within these sources is often public and involves the entire faith community.

The early church fathers argued that water baptism served two primary purposes: (1) baptism is how one receives forgiveness of sins, and (2) baptism is how one enters the faith community. The Didache (early second century), Justin Martyr (d. 165), Tertullian (d. 240), and Origen (d. 253) show drastic hermeneutical shifts among Christian interpretations of baptism within the first 150 years of the church—i.e., a lessening of the death and resurrection imagery present in Paul and a heightening role of the faith community and pre-baptismal works.[3]

Salvation is *in Christ*. Therefore, the moment one is "baptized into Christ" (Rom 6:1–4) becomes the moment of incorporation. Every conversion narrative in Acts follows this pattern: hearing the gospel message, believing the message, and being baptized immediately. There is no example

---

2. Ferguson, *Baptism*, 854.

3. For a more thorough analysis of baptism in the early church fathers, see Houston, "Similar but Different," 231–38.

in the New Testament of converts accepting Jesus into their hearts, nor are there any examples of converts praying to receive salvation. Further, no text in the New Testament after the formation of the church portrays unbaptized disciples. When unusual events precede baptism, such as Cornelius's reception of the Spirit before his baptism, the apostles treat the phenomenon as an exception rather than the norm and demand immediate sacramental completion (cf. Acts 10:47–48).

ADDRESSING CALVINIST OBJECTIONS

Calvinists often cite the thief on the cross as proof that baptism is not necessary for salvation. The counterargument notes that Christian baptism in the triune name (Matt 28:19) was not instituted until after the resurrection of Jesus; the thief belongs to the old covenant, which Jesus fulfills. Additionally, others point to Paul's statement that he was sent "not to baptize but to preach the gospel" (1 Cor 1:17) as proof that Paul did not highly value baptism. Yet, Paul's words target the unholy attitude of the divisive Christians in Corinth, not baptism's insignificance. In fact, Paul admits to baptizing entire households in Corinth (1 Cor 1:14–16). Still others worry that making baptism essential for salvation makes salvation works-based. Paul answers this critique when he states, "In baptism you were raised through faith in the powerful working of God" (Col 2:12). The efficacy, then, is God's, not ours.

WEIGHING THE TWO POSITIONS

Both traditions confess that salvation results from divine grace. Each baptizes in the name of the Father, Son, and Spirit. Each warns baptized persons that unrepentant sin endangers the soul. The division lies in whether God binds saving grace to the moment of immersion or seals a grace bestowed at the Spirit's sovereign discretion without a response of obedience. Calvin feared that strict sacramental necessity would restrain God's sovereignty. In a Calvinist congregation, baptism functions chiefly as a retrospective assurance in which one may look back to one's baptism and remember the promise of salvation already given irresistibly. In churches that treat the rite as necessary for salvation, baptism is the decisive forward step—the burial and birth that marks one's entrance into the body of Christ. The former argues that justification comes by faith alone, whereas the latter anchors faith in a tangible moment of obedience.

CONCLUSION

Scripture teaches that baptism is the means by which sins are washed away and new creation in Christ begins. The debate concerning baptism between Calvinists and non-Calvinists is unlikely to disappear any time soon because it touches the nerve of the gospel itself. The larger question is, "How do we receive grace?" Yet the conversation need not degenerate into misrepresentation of the truth. Without baptism, one cannot receive forgiveness of sins. Without forgiveness, one cannot be justified. Without justification, one must receive the justice of God, which is condemnation. Baptism is essential.

20

Where I Stand with Calvinism

THE PROTESTANT REFORMATION OF the sixteenth century and beyond rightly broke away from the unbiblical traditions of Catholicism. The Catholic Church at the time was abusing its power by forcing the purchases of indulgences and refusing to allow the public to read and interpret Scripture for themselves. Men such as John Wycliff, William Tyndale, and Martin Luther were key in "reforming" the church to what it needed to be. Getting the Bible in the hands of the people was paramount to Christianity's revival and survival.

However, the rightful break from penance and relics led the Reformers down a rabbit hole with the doctrine of grace. Grace is essential and certainly a biblical doctrine, but debate abounds even today on the purpose of grace and how one accesses it. During his early years as an Augustinian friar in Erfurt and Wittenberg, Martin Luther was consumed by a crushing fear of judgment, which drove him into an obsessive routine of confession. Luther would often spend up to six hours a day in the confessional revisiting every conceivable sin only to fear he had omitted some and remain uncertain of absolution.[1] Luther then read the book of Romans where he saw that the grace of God is given in Jesus Christ to those who place their faith in him (Rom 5:1–11). Additionally, Luther coupled Romans with Eph 2:8 where Paul states that believers are saved by grace through faith. To be sure,

---

1. See Marius, *Martin Luther*, 43–54.

Luther's movement away from the Catholic Church was not intended to begin a new religious group. Luther only wanted to publicly discuss what he perceived to be wrong with the theology and doctrine of his time. In this sense, I share a similar passion with Luther. As I have demonstrated in this book, many of the doctrines that many good, moral, and studious people accept as "true" cannot be upheld by Scripture. Thus, the only response is to have another movement—a movement that brings these issues into the public square.

Beyond issues of grace, faith, mercy, baptism, and assurance stand the issues of the foreknowledge and sovereignty of God. If God infallibly knows every future act, how can free will exist? If God meticulously governs the course of history, how can humans be morally responsible? From the patristic period through the Middle Ages, most Christian thinkers adopted a broadly "classical" model suggesting that God is eternal, immutable, simple, and omniscient. Thus, the entire sweep of history is present to him in a single, timeless act of knowing. Augustine famously pictured God "standing outside time" so that past, present, and future are equally transparent to his gaze (*Confessions* 11). Boethius refined the account by stating that God's knowledge is not foreseen but "vision," i.e., an ever-present intuition of all events, which therefore does not coerce human choices.[2]

Reformed theologians integrated this atemporal knowledge with a strong doctrine of providence. John Calvin insisted that God "so arranges all things that nothing happens without his counsel" (*Institutes* 1.16.3–4) while nevertheless holding humans responsible for their voluntary sins—a clear philosophical contradiction. Jonathan Edwards later supplied a philosophical defense, arguing that moral responsibility is compatible with determinism so long as actions arise from one's motives.[3] Jacobus Arminius (d. 1609) accepted the timeless knowledge of classical theism but rejected divine determinism. God, he maintained, foreknows future free acts because they will occur, not because he decrees them.[4] This "simple foreknowledge" allows genuine libertarian freedom—agents could have done otherwise—while preserving divine omniscience. But if God merely foresees free choices then he cannot guarantee a particular outcome in history, which raises questions about prophecy, providence, and answered prayer.

---

2. See Boethius, *Theological Tractates*.
3. See Edwards, *Freedom of the Will*, 327.
4. Arminius, *Declaration of the Sentiments*, 248.

Section Two

Luis de Molina (1535–1600) proposed a mediating solution grounded in God's *scientia media*—knowledge of what any free creature *would* do in any possible set of circumstances. Thus, God's sovereignty is preserved and free will is safeguarded. Modern Molinists—most notably William Lane Craig and Thomas Flint—argue that middle knowledge explains specific providence without collapsing into determinism.

Open theists push the debate further, contending that future free acts are *indeterminate even for God* because they do not yet exist to be known. God knows everything that can be known—past, present, and all possibilities—but the future is necessarily "open." Clark Pinnock, John Sanders, and William Hasker appeal to biblical portraits of God who tests (Gen 22), changes his mind (Exod 33), or regrets prior actions (Gen 6), insisting that a responsive, relational deity fits Scripture better than an immutable, blueprint-governing sovereign.

Process theologians such as Charles Hartshorne go still further in redefining the classical doctrine of God by proposing a dipolar conception of divinity in which God possesses both a changeless, abstract pole and a dynamic, relational pole. In this model, God does not remain omniscient in the traditional sense but rather grows in knowledge and power in tandem with the unfolding of the world. Divine foreknowledge is reinterpreted as a "prehension" of all possible outcomes to describe God's intimate but open-ended awareness of the world's becoming.[5] God influences creation by persuasion rather than coercion, and the future remains genuinely undetermined even for God. However, most theologians have rejected this model as incompatible with core doctrines of the Christian faith, particularly *creatio ex nihilo*, omnipotence, and the bodily resurrection of Christ and believers. Critics argue that a God who cannot guarantee the triumph of good or the final redemption of creation is not the God revealed in Scripture.

The fundamental issue rests with God's relationship to time and human responsibility. Does God transcend temporal succession (atemporalism) or endure through it (temporalism)? Many open theists and process theologians adopt divine temporality while classical and Reformed thinkers largely retain timelessness. Further, can agents be blameworthy if their choices are part of an infallible decree? Compatibilists say yes—freedom is acting according to one's desires while libertarians object. The debate's longevity suggests that no single model eliminates every challenge. The best proposals therefore combine intellectual rigor with humility. Gregory

---

5. For more on Harsthorne's views, see Hartshorne, *Divine Relativity*, 1–59.

Where I Stand with Calvinism

of Nyssa's warning remains apt: "Every concept forming about God is an idol."[6] No one can claim to exhaust the mystery of the one "who works all things according to the counsel of his will" (Eph 1:11).

Whether one sides with Augustine, Molina, or Sanders, the task of theology is to explore the grandeur of God's wisdom and the dignity of his image bearers' freedom. God is sovereign. But God so loved the world that he sent his Son (John 3:16). God's love for the world provides salvific hope to all. God desires all to be saved and come to a knowledge of truth (1 Tim 2:4). In this sense, the doctrine of limited atonement is incompatible with Scripture. Many will freely reject the free gift of God, but the gift is offered and available should they desire to receive it.

My primary issue with Calvinism is that their doctrines can only stand if its premise of God's sovereignty and foreknowledge are true. I am convinced that these doctrines do not fit with the truth of free will. Either humanity has free will, and Calvinism is wrong, or humanity does not have free will, and Calvinism is right, thus making love nonexistent and God the author of evil.

Perhaps I have been harsher toward Calvinism than toward Catholicism in the earlier discussion. This is not out of disregard for the immense contributions of the Reformed tradition. Because it offers so many contributions to biblical interpretation and theology, it demands scrutiny. While I have attempted to critique what I believe are significant theological flaws—particularly regarding divine determinism, limited atonement, and irresistible grace—I remain unconvinced by the central claims of Calvinism. Nevertheless, I do not dismiss the value of the Reformation movement as a whole. On the contrary, I am deeply indebted to the Reformers for their unwavering commitment to Scripture, their courage in confronting corruption, and their reassertion of the gospel's clarity and sufficiency. In a sense, that is what I am trying to do in this book.

To be sure, I find common ground with Martin Luther's insistence that salvation does not arise from human works apart from Christ. Similarly, I appreciate John Calvin's emphasis on grace as the operative and saving force in the life of the believer. My disagreement lies not with the priority or necessity of grace, but with its application as limited, coercive, or devoid of human response. In short, while I reject many aspects of Calvinism, I affirm the broader Protestant witness that salvation is not based in relics or penance but is found in Christ by grace through faith realized in obedience.

---

6. Gregory, *Life of Moses* 2.163.

21

Conclusion

THE PRECEDING CHAPTERS HAVE carried us through a demanding but necessary conversation first with Rome, then with Wittenberg and Geneva. We have asked whether the Roman magisterium is identical with the "one, holy, universal and apostolic church," and whether the Protestant cry of *sola gratia* and *sola fide* offers a complete account of salvation. Along the way we have returned repeatedly to a single touchstone—the New Testament's picture of the people of God—and have tested every later development against that canon. What remains is to pursue three tasks: (1) to synthesize the book's findings under the rubric of unity and authority, (2) to propose a retrieval of the earliest church as the most viable horizon for future ecumenical conversation, and (3) to suggest a practical agenda for seekers who wish to be neither Roman Catholic nor Calvinist but simply—and radically—Christian.

Both Catholicism and the Reformation confess one visible church, yet each is implicated in the fragmentation that now disfigures Christ's body. Rome's boast of structural unity falters when measured against the liturgical and moral fissures that divide traditionalists, progressives, and national bishops' conferences. Protestantism, for its part, achieved a liberation of conscience only to multiply denominations, a pluralism that sits uneasily beside Jesus's high priestly prayer for oneness in John 17.

I also presented a dialogue between proposed sources of authority. Catholics elevate capital-"T" Tradition alongside Scripture (including the

Conclusion

apocrypha) and entrust its interpretation to the magisterium. Calvinists champion *sola scriptura* with a biblical canon of sixty-six books but often replace conciliar oversight with individual—or, in practice, confessional—readings that are no less tradition-bound. This book's sustained critique is that both models outrun the evidence of the first two Christian centuries in which authority functioned under a plurality of elders and a non-confessional and non-creedal rule of faith. The conclusion is not to abandon tradition but to relocate it. Tradition is the church's memory in service of Scripture, never its rival.

Catholicism rightly guards baptismal regeneration and eucharistic observance, yet binds them to an ontology of transubstantiation and a clerical class. Conversely, many Reformed churches preserve Christological orthodoxy but evacuate baptism of its New Testament soteriological weight by treating it as retrospective rather than the Spirit's ordinary means of incorporation. The present study argues that baptism into Christ is both necessary and sufficient for forgiveness and that the Lord's Supper is a memorial saturated with the real presence of Christ but not a fresh sacrifice in which the emblems miraculously change into the flesh and blood of Jesus.

The sacrament of weekly Communion functions as both glue and guardrail. It gathers the faithful around the cross in humility, while self-examination (1 Cor 11:26) disciplines unrepentant sin. A church that unites around the table each Sunday is discipled into unity. A church that fences the table against unfaithfulness protects holiness. This vision holds sacrament and sanctity together without resorting to theories foreign to Scripture. The gospel's credibility is tethered to the church's integrity (John 17:21).

If neither Rome's magisterium nor Geneva's confessions can exhaust the church's identity, where should we look? The answer offered throughout this book is the prototypical church that flourished from Pentecost to the end of the first century. That community exhibited five features that constitute a blueprint for catholicity without clericalism.

First, congregations of the first-century church were governed by a plurality of elders and deacons, not a monarchical bishop or distant pontiff. Second, the earliest believers met each Lord's Day for Scripture, prayer, a cappella praise in song, and the breaking of bread (i.e., the Lord's Supper). Third, conversion in the first-century church followed the triadic pattern of faith, repentance, and immediate immersion for the forgiveness of sins, making baptism the locus of justification, adoption, and new creation. Fourth, salvation once received could be forfeited by apostasy; yet, assurance was real for those who continued to "walk in the light" (1 John 1:7). Finally, corporate worship anticipated the marriage supper of the Lamb and called the community to a unity that foreshadows its eschatological perfection. Recovering these practices is a strategic retrieval aimed at healing fractures of modern Christianity. Denominationalism, whether within Catholicism or Protestantism, wounds our witness.

DOES THE TRUE CHURCH OF JESUS CHRIST EXIST TODAY?

The present study has evaluated the doctrines of the two most prominent theological entities in Christianity today. Having evaluated these doctrines (and leaving many others without an evaluation for sake of space), one may wonder if the true, authentic church exists today. The answer, I think, is yes. If it does, what are its hallmarks? How can we become a part of it?

The true church of Jesus Christ must be set on the foundations of the apostles and prophets of which Jesus is the cornerstone (Eph 2:20). There can be no authority in the church other than the crucified and risen Lord and the inspired word of God. Certainly, tradition has its place; however, those things that are not rooted in the Bible alone cannot stand the scrutiny of Scripture's standard. For example, most (but certainly not all) Christians today meet in buildings designated for worship and other spiritual activity. But what if Christians met elsewhere? Scripture does not command that Christians meet in a cathedral or church building. It does, however, command that Christians meet (Heb 10:25). One may also think about the use of a hymnal. The Bible does not command such use, but it does command singing (Eph 5:19; Col 3:16).

The true church of Jesus will acknowledge baptism as the means by which sins are forgiven and salvation is received (Acts 2:28; 22:16; 1 Pet 3:21). Any congregation that denies baptism's significance and essentiality is not—according to Scripture—aligned with the true church of Jesus. Baptism is not a symbol. It is the very act that brings the sinner into saved communion with the Father, justified by the blood of Jesus. Though many theologians today seek to separate the doctrines of faith, grace, love, mercy, and baptism, I am convinced that the New Testament does not do this. The New Testament nowhere presents "grace alone" or "faith alone" as isolated mechanisms of salvation. Rather, faith and grace converge in the

Conclusion

act of baptism, which functions as the moment wherein the believer enters into union with Christ and thus receives forgiveness of sins.

The true church of Jesus must worship according to the practices of the earliest church. The church today is called to pattern its worship according to the divinely revealed standard established by the first-century church in the New Testament. The earliest apostolic church under the direct guidance of the Holy Spirit offers the normative model for Christian worship wherein practices such as prayer, the Lord's Supper, a cappella congregational singing, the reading and teaching of Scripture, and giving were central (Acts 2:42; 1 Cor 14:26; Col 3:16). To depart from this pattern is to risk substituting human innovation for divine instruction. Since Christ is the head of the church (Eph 1:22–23), worship must remain Christocentric. In this way, the true church remains rooted in the unchanging will of God, expressed once for all through the apostles (Jude 3).

The true church of Jesus will be organized according to the pattern set forth in Scripture. It will have a plurality of elders who shepherd the flock and deacons who serve the flock according to the qualities mentioned in 1 Tim 3:1–13 and Titus 1:5–9 respectively. It will have men as the spiritual leaders of the worship service and of congregational order (1 Cor 14:34; 1 Tim 2:11). Its preacher will preach the word, being ready in season and out of season (2 Tim 4:2). It will seek not to please the culture but to submit reverently to the authority of Christ, who alone has the right to govern his church (Col 1:18). Any departure from this apostolic model is a deviation from the will of God.

The true church of Jesus will celebrate the Lord's Supper on every first day of the week according to the example of the early church found in Scripture. Congregations that only participate in communion on Easter, Christmas, quarterly, or monthly do not follow the example set by the first-century church. In fact, Paul's words in 1 Cor 11:26—"for as often as you eat this bread and drink this cup"—imply a more frequent partaking of the Lord's Supper, not less. On the other hand, any teaching that proclaims Christ's continual sacrifice as a victim is not according to the standard of the New Testament church. Catholic eucharistic adoration begins with the hymn "O Salutaris Hostia," composed by Thomas Aquinas. The first line reads in English, "O saving Victim." Yet, Christ fervently states that he is *not* a victim! No one takes his life; he freely laid it down (John 10:18). The true church will acknowledge and glory in Christ's once-for-all sacrifice.

Conclusion

The true church of Jesus will meet on the first day of the week. The church meets on Sunday because it is theologically grounded in the resurrection of Jesus Christ, which occurred on the first day of the week (Matt 28:1; Mark 16:2; Luke 24:1; John 20:1). This day, often referred to in early Christian literature as "the Lord's Day" (cf. Rev 1:10), holds special significance as the beginning of the new creation inaugurated by Christ's victory over death. The apostles and the early church modeled this practice by assembling on the first day of the week to break bread (Acts 20:7), to contribute financially to the needs of the saints (1 Cor 16:1–2), and to receive teaching. To gather on Sunday is not a matter of tradition, but of devotion. It is a weekly proclamation of the resurrection, a visible expression of eschatological hope, and an obedient participation in the apostolic pattern of worship.

The true church of Jesus will submit to the authority of the Bible as the inspired and infallible word of God. Divine inspiration must be limited to the original authors and their autographs. Inerrancy and infallibility do not rest with the copies of Scripture, and authority does not rest with the scribe who copied it. Each of these qualities rest with God who has revealed himself via written word. His revelation is without error. Because God reveals himself without error, the other things that God reveals (e.g., his Son, his will, his plan of salvation) are also without error. Therefore, the true church of Jesus must accept and uphold that the Bible alone is the word of God given to his creation.

Because the Bible is the inspired word of God, the true church of Jesus must reject any man-made documents as infallible or authoritative to the same level as Scripture. The true church will reject creedal confessions as necessary for salvation and ordination not because they are untrue or unnecessary but because they are always subordinate to the authority of Scripture. Human confessions and creeds, however well intentioned, ultimately stand in the way of true Christian unity and biblical authority. In 1803, Barton W. Stone publicly rejected the Westminster Confession of Faith by declaring that it could not bind the conscience or govern the church with the same authority as Scripture.[1] He argued that creeds often promoted division, elevated theological systems above the plain teaching of the Bible, and imposed human interpretations as tests of fellowship. For Stone, the only legitimate foundation for the church was the New Testament itself. His stance marked a clear departure from creedal allegiance.

---

1. Boring, *Disciples and the Bible*, 17.

CONCLUSION

Finally, the true church of Jesus will acknowledge that there is only *one* church of Jesus Christ. We are either in it, or we are not. Christ established a singular body over which he alone is its head (Eph 1:22–23; 4:4–5). Entrance into Christ's body is not determined by denominational affiliation or by human tradition but only by obedience to the good and beautiful gospel message. Obedience to that message appears as faith in Christ, repentance of sins, confession that Jesus is the Son of God, and baptism for the remission of sins (Acts 2:38; Gal 3:27). These are not separated but are interconnected to bring about salvation. Based on one's obedience to the gospel, the Lord adds that one to his church (Acts 2:47). To affirm the existence of multiple, divergent bodies as equally valid expressions of Christ's church is to deny the unity of the one body. The true church will not seek religious pluralism but will return wholly to the apostolic faith once for all delivered to the saints (Jude 3).

BECOMING THE CHURCH WE SEEK

We stand at an ecclesiological crossroads. Rome invites us to submit to an infallible magisterium. Geneva offers a confessional rationalism that often drifts into individualism. The pages of this book have mapped a third way: a biblically ordered, historically conscious, and missionally urgent church. Such a church will be recognizably ancient—immersing believers in baptism (Acts 2:38; 1 Pet 3:21), taking of the Lord's Supper each first day of the week (Acts 20:7), singing without mechanical aid (Eph 5:18–19; Col 3:16), and shepherded by a plurality of qualified elders (Acts 14:23; 1 Tim 3). Let us therefore "contend for the faith once for all delivered to the saints" (Jude 3), yet do so with charity that invites all to the waters of rebirth. Let congregations become laboratories of unity where all may taste the simplicity and power of true apostolic Christianity. Let its scholars labor in the sources, its preachers proclaim grace suffused with obedience, and its members embody a holiness that neither despairs under legalism nor presumes upon cheap grace.

Should we succeed, the watching world may glimpse again the radiant bride "without spot or wrinkle" for whom Christ died (Eph 5:27). And perhaps, in God's mercy, the long-divided household of faith will rediscover its baptismal name: not Catholic, not Calvinist, but Christ's.

Bibliography

Aquinas, Thomas. *Summa Theologiae*. Translated by the Fathers of the English Dominican Province. New York: Benziger Brothers, 1947.
Aristotle. *Metaphysics*. Translated by Hugh Tredennick. 2 vols. LCL. Cambridge, MA: Harvard University Press, 1933–35.
Arminius, Jacobus. *A Declaration of the Sentiments of Arminius*. In *The Writings of James Arminius* 3, translated by James Nichols and W. R. Bagnall. Grand Rapids: Baker, 1986.
———. *The Works of Jacobus Arminius*. Translated by James E. Tomson. 3 vols. Grand Rapids: Baker, 1986.
Augustine. *Answer to Faustus, a Manichean*. Translated by Richard Stothert. In *Nicene and Post-Nicene Fathers*, 1st ser., edited by Philip Schaff, 4:155–345. Repr., Peabody, MA: Hendrickson, 1994.
———. *Answer to the Pelagians 4*. Edited by John E. Rotelle. Translated by Roland J. Teske. Vol. 1/23 of *The Works of Saint Augustine: A Translation for the 21st Century*. Hyde Park, NY: New City, 1999.
———. *The City of God*. Translated by Marcus Dods. In *Nicene and Post-Nicene Fathers*, 1st ser., edited by Philip Schaff, 2:1–511. Repr., Peabody, MA: Hendrickson, 1994.
———. *On the Spirit and the Letter*. Translated and edited by W. J. Sparrow-Simpson. *Translations of Christian Literature Latin Texts*, 2nd ser. New York: Macmillan, 1925.
Bailey, D. S. *The Petrine Claims*. London: SCM, 1960.
Bailey, Randall. *Improving Your Prayer Life Through a Study of the Psalter*. Eugene, OR: Wipf & Stock, 2021.
Barth, Karl. *The Doctrine of God*. Vol. 2 of *Church Dogmatics*, edited by G. W. Bromiley and T. F. Torrance, translated by G. W. Bromiley et al. Edinburgh: T. & T. Clark, 1957.
Bavinck, Herman. *Sin and Salvation in Christ*. Edited by John Bolt. Translated by John Vriend. Vol. 3/4 of *Reformed Dogmatics*. Grand Rapids: Baker Academic, 2006.
Berkhof, Louis. *Systematic Theology*. Grand Rapids: Eerdmans, 1941.
Boethius. *Theological Tractates. The Consolation of Philosophy*. Translated by S. J. Tester. LCL. Cambridge, MA: Harvard University Press, 1973.
Bonhoeffer, Dietrich. *The Cost of Discipleship*. Translated by R. H. Fuller. Rev. ed. London: SCM, 2001.
Boring, Eugene. *Disciples and the Bible: A History of Disciples Biblical Interpretation in North America*. St. Louis, MO: Chalice, 1997.

Bibliography

Bruce, F. F. *The Book of the Acts*. NICNT. Grand Rapids: Eerdmans, 1988.

Calvin, John. *Institutes of the Christian Religion*. Edited by John T. McNeill. Translated by Ford Lewis Battles. 2 vols. Philadelphia: Westminster, 1960.

———. *A Treatise on Relics*. Translated by Valerian Krasinski. London: Longmans, Green and Co., 1844.

Campbell, Alexander. "An Address on the Lord's Supper." *Christian Baptist* 3.12 (1827) 95–98.

Clement of Alexandria. *Paedagogus (The Instructor)*. In *The Ante-Nicene Fathers*, edited by Alexander Roberts and James Donaldson, 2:151–377. Buffalo, NY: Christian Literature, 1885.

Congregation for the Causes of Saints. *Sanctorum Mater: Instruction for Conducting Diocesan or Eparchial Inquiries in the Causes of Saints*. Vatican City: Libreria Editrice Vaticana, 2007.

Congregation for Divine Worship and the Discipline of the Sacraments. *Directory on Popular Piety and the Liturgy: Principles and Guidelines*. Vatican City: Libreria Editrice Vaticana, 2001.

Cottrell, Jack. *The Faith Once for All: Biblical Doctrine for Today*. Joplin, MO: College Press, 2002.

Council of Trent. *Decree on Indulgences*. In *The Canons and Decrees of the Council of Trent*, edited and translated by H. J. Schroeder, 230–31. Rockford, IL: TAN, 1978.

Cyril of Jerusalem. *Catechetical Lectures*. Translated by Edward Yarnold. In *Early Christian Fathers*, edited by Cyril C. Richardson, 205–384. New York: Macmillan, 1970.

Danker, Frederick W., et al. *Greek-English Lexicon of the New Testament and Other Early Christian Literature*. 3rd ed. Chicago: University of Chicago Press, 2000.

Edwards, Jonathan. *Freedom of the Will*. Edited by Paul Ramsey. The Works of Jonathan Edwards 1. New Haven, CT: Yale University Press, 1957.

Ehrman, Bart D., ed. and trans. "Didache." In *The Apostolic Fathers* 1, 405–515. 2nd ed. LCL. Cambridge, MA: Harvard University Press, 2003.

———, ed. and trans. *Martyrdom of Polycarp*. In *The Apostolic Fathers* 2, 325–403. 2nd ed. LCL. Cambridge, MA: Harvard University Press, 2003.

Eusebius. *Commentary on the Psalms*. In *Patrologia Graeca*, edited by J. P. Migne, 23:1172. Paris: Imprimerie Catholique, 1857.

Ferguson, Everett. *Baptism in the Early Church*. Grand Rapids: Eerdmans, 2009.

———. *The Rule of Faith: A Guide*. Eugene, OR: Cascade, 2015.

Fradd, Matt. "7 Things Protestants Misunderstand About Christianity (Dr. John Bergsma) | Ep. 523." YouTube. May 7, 2025. Video, 01:23–02:06. https://www.youtube.com/watch?v=qIYoaVxK44E&t=5010s.

Francis. *Amoris Laetitia (The Joy of Love): Post-Synodal Apostolic Exhortation on Love in the Family*. Vatican City: Libreria Editrice Vaticana, 2016.

———. *The Name of God Is Mercy: A Conversation with Andrea Tornielli*. Translated by Oonagh Stransky. New York: Random House, 2016.

Galen. *De naturalibus facultatibus*. In *Claudii Galeni Opera Omnia*, edited by C. G. Kühn, 2:1–182. Leipzig: Cnobloch, 1821.

Garland, David. "The Lord's Prayer in the Gospel of Matthew." *Review and Expositor* 89 (1992) 215–28.

Gregory. *The Life of Moses*. Translated by Abraham J. Malherbe and Everett Ferguson. Classics of Western Spirituality. New York: Paulist, 1978.

Bibliography

Hahn, Scott. *The Lamb's Supper: The Mass as Heaven on Earth*. New York: Doubleday, 1999.

Hartshorne, Charles. *The Divine Relativity: A Social Conception of God*. New Haven, CT: Yale University Press, 1948.

Hughes, Philip. *A History of the Church* 1. London: Sheed & Ward, 1947.

Horton, Michael. *The Christian Faith: A Systematic Theology for Pilgrims on the Way*. Grand Rapids: Zondervan, 2011.

Houston, Joshua. "Similar but Different: Exploring the Hermeneutical Shift of Baptism Within the Early Church." *ResQ* 64 (2022) 231–38.

Ignatius. *Letter to the Ephesians*. Translated by Alexander Roberts and James Donaldson. In *The Ante-Nicene Fathers*, edited by Alexander Roberts and James Donaldson, 1:85–103. Buffalo, NY: Christian Literature, 1885.

———. *Letter to the Smyrnaeans*. In *The Apostolic Fathers* 1, edited and translated by Bart D. Ehrman, 269–307. 2nd ed. LCL. Cambridge, MA: Harvard University Press, 2003.

———. *Letter to the Trallians*. Translated by Alexander Roberts and James Donaldson. In *The Ante-Nicene Fathers*, edited by Alexander Roberts and James Donaldson, 1:104–14. Buffalo, NY: Christian Literature, 1885.

Instone-Brewer, David. *Divorce and Remarriage in the Church*. Downers Grove, IL: InterVarsity, 2003.

Irenaeus. *Against Heresies*. Translated by Alexander Roberts and William Rambaut. In *The Ante-Nicene Fathers*, edited by Alexander Roberts and James Donaldson, 1:315–563. Buffalo, NY: Christian Literature, 1885.

Jerome. "Letter 46 (to Oceanus)." Translated by Alexander Roberts. In *Nicene and Post-Nicene Fathers*, 2nd ser., edited by Philip Schaff, 6:420–21. Repr., Peabody, MA: Hendrickson, 1994.

John of Damascus. *On the Dormition of Mary: Early Patristic Homilies*. Edited and translated by Brian E. Daley. Popular Patristics, 18th ser. Crestwood, NY: St. Vladimir's Seminary Press, 1998.

Justin Martyr. *The First Apology*. Translated by Alexander Roberts and James Donaldson. In *The Ante-Nicene Fathers*, edited by Alexander Roberts and James Donaldson, 1:185–246. Buffalo, NY: Christian Literature, 1885.

Kelly, J. N. D. *Early Christian Creeds*. 3rd ed. New York: Continuum, 1972.

———. *Early Christian Doctrines*. 5th ed. San Francisco: HarperOne, 1978.

Leith, J. H., ed. *Heidelberg Catechism*. In *The Confessions of the Reformed Church*, 64–66. Louisville: Westminster John Knox, 2000.

Lightfoot, J. B. *The Apostolic Fathers: Comprising the Epistles (Genuine and Spurious) of Clement of Rome, the Epistles of S. Ignatius, the Epistle of S. Polycarp, the Martyrdom of S. Polycarp, the Teaching of the Apostles, the Epistle of Barnabas, the Shepherd of Hermas, the Epistle to Diognetus, the Fragments of Papias, the Reliques of the Elders Preserved in Irenaeus*. 2 vols. London: Macmillan, 1891.

Luther, Martin. *Disputation on the Power and Efficacy of Indulgences (The 95 Theses)*. Translated by Harold J. Grimm. In *Career of the Reformer 1*, edited by Harold J. Grimm, 25–33. Vol. 31/55 of *Luther's Works*. Philadelphia: Fortress, 1957.

———. *Large Catechism*. In *Luther's Works* 35, edited by Jaroslav Pelikan and Helmut T. Lehmann, translated by Concordia Publishing House, 337–522. St. Louis, MO: Concordia, 1959.

———. *On the Freedom of a Christian*. In *Career of the Reformer I*, edited by Harold J. Grimm, 327–77. Vol. 31 of *Luther's Works*. Philadelphia: Muhlenberg, 1957.

Bibliography

———. *Preface to the Complete Edition of Luther's Latin Writings (1545)*. Translated by Lewis W. Spitz. In *Career of the Reformer IV*, edited by Lewis W. Spitz, 323–38. Vol. 34 of *Luther's Works*. Philadelphia: Muhlenberg, 1960.

———. *Small Catechism*. Edited by Timothy J. Wengert. Minneapolis: Fortress, 2017.

———. *Table Talk*. Edited and translated by Theodore G. Tappert. Vol. 54/55 of *Luther's Works*. Philadelphia: Fortress, 1967.

Luz, Ulrich. *Matthew 1—7: A Commentary*. Translated by W. C. Linss. Minneapolis: Augsburg, 1989.

Marius, Richard. *Martin Luther: The Christian Between God and Death*. Cambridge, MA: Harvard University Press, 1999.

McBrien, Richard. *Lives of the Popes*. San Francisco: HarperSanFrancisco, 1997.

McCormack, Bruce. *Karl Barth's Theology: A Prelude to Evangelical Catholicism*. Oxford: Oxford University Press, 2000.

McGrath, Alister. *Christian Theology: An Introduction*. 7th ed. Oxford: Wiley-Blackwell, 2020.

———. *Reformation Thought: An Introduction*. 3rd ed. Oxford: Wiley-Blackwell, 2012.

McNeile, A. H. *The Gospel According to St. Matthew*. New York: Macmillan, 1955.

Mershman, Francis. "Sts. Gervasius and Protasius." In *Catholic Encyclopedia* 6. New York: Robert Appleton Company, 1909. http://www.newadvent.org/cathen/06537a.htm.

Michaels, J. Ramsey. *Revelation*. The IVP New Testament Commentary Series. Downers Grove, IL: InterVarsity, 1997.

Nolland, John. *The Gospel of Matthew*. Grand Rapids: Eerdmans, 2005.

O'Connor, Flannery. *The Habit of Being: Letters of Flannery O'Connor*. Edited by Sally Fitzgerald. New York: Farrar, Straus and Giroux, 1979.

Origen. *Homilies on Jeremiah*. Translated by John Clark Smith. FC 97. Washington, DC: Catholic University of America Press, 1998.

Paul VI. *Humanae Vitae (Of Human Life): Encyclical on the Regulation of Birth*. Vatican City: Libreria Editrice Vaticana, 1968.

Paul, John II. *Ordinatio Sacerdotalis (Apostolic Letter on the Reservation of Priestly Ordination to Men Alone)*. Vatican City: Libreria Editrice Vaticana, 1994.

———. *Rosarium Virginis Mariae: Apostolic Letter on the Most Holy Rosary*. Vatican City: Libreria Editrice Vaticana, 2002.

Pettigrove, Glen. "Forgiveness and Interpretation." *JRE* 35 (2007) 430.

Picirilli, Robert E. *Grace, Faith, Free Will*. Nashville: Randall House, 2002.

Pliny the Younger. *Letters*. Translated by Betty Radice. In *The Letters of the Younger Pliny*, 293–95. Rev. ed. London: Penguin Classics, 2003.

Polycarp. "Epistle to the Philippians." Translated by Alexander Roberts and James Donaldson. In *The Ante-Nicene Fathers*, edited by Alexander Roberts and James Donaldson, 1:99–112. Buffalo, NY: Christian Literature, 1885.

Pseudo-Melito. *The Passing of the Virgin: Transitus Mariae*. In *New Testament Apocrypha, Volume 1: Gospels and Related Writings*, edited by Bart D. Ehrman and Zlatko Pleše, 475–85. Cambridge, MA: Harvard University Press, 2011.

Pliny the Younger. *Letters*. In *The Letters of the Younger Pliny*, translated by Betty Radice. LCL 52. Cambridge, MA: Harvard University Press, 1969.

Polybius. *The Histories*. Translated by W. R. Paton. 6 vols. LCL. Cambridge, MA: Harvard University Press, 1922–27.

Rogers, Cleon Jr., and Cleon Rogers III. *The New Linguistic and Exegetical Key to the Greek New Testament*. Grand Rapids: Zondervan, 1998.

Bibliography

Synod of Dort. *The Canons of Dort*. In *The Creeds of Christendom*, edited by Philip Schaff, 3:581–97. 3rd ed. Grand Rapids: Baker, 1983.

Tanner, Norman P., ed. "Fourth Lateran Council, 1215." In *Decrees of the Ecumenical Councils*, 1:159–246. Washington, DC: Georgetown University Press, 1990.

Tertullian. *De corona militis (The Crown)*. In *Tertullian: Disciplinary, Moral and Ascetical Works*, translated by Rudolph Arbesmann et al., 94–121. FC 40. Washington, DC: Catholic University of America Press, 1959.

———. *Prescription Against Heretics*. Translated by Peter Holmes. In *The Ante-Nicene Fathers*, edited by Alexander Roberts and James Donaldson, 3:243–71. Buffalo, NY: Christian Literature, 1885.

Thurston, Herbert. "Confraternity of the Holy Rosary." *Catholic Encyclopedia* 13. New York: Robert Appleton, 1912.

Turretin, Francis. *Institutes of Elenctic Theology* 2:587–613. Edited by James T. Dennison. Translated by George M. Giger. 3 vols. Phillipsburg, NJ: Presbyterian and Reformed, 1992–97.

Tyndale, William. *The Works of the English Reformers: William Tyndale and John Frith* 1. Edited by Thomas Russell. London: Ebenezer Palmer, 1831.

United States Catholic Conference. *Catechism of the Catholic Church*. Washington, DC: Libreria Editrice Vaticana, 1994.

Ursinus, Zacharias, and Caspar Olevianus. "The Heidelberg Catechism." In *Reformed Confessions of the 16th and 17th Centuries in English Translation, Volume 2: 1552–1566*, edited and translated by James T. Dennison Jr., 775–828. Grand Rapids: Reformation Heritage, 2010.

Vatican Council I. "*Pastor Aeternus* (Dogmatic Constitution on the Church of Christ)." In *Decrees of the Ecumenical Councils*, edited by Norman P. Tanner, 2:812–35. Washington, DC: Georgetown University Press, 1990.

Vatican II. "*Lumen Gentium* (Dogmatic Constitution on the Church)." In *Vatican Council II: The Conciliar and Post Conciliar Documents*, edited by Austin Flannery, 350–428. Northport, NY: Costello, 1996.

Warfield, Benjamin B. "On the Biblical Notion of 'Renewal.'" In *Biblical and Theological Studies*, edited by Samuel G. Craig, 351–74. Philadelphia: Presbyterian and Reformed, 1952.

———. "Predestination." In *Biblical and Theological Studies*, edited by Samuel G. Craig, 270–333. Philadelphia: Presbyterian and Reformed, 1952.

Westminster Assembly. *The Westminster Confession of Faith*. 3rd ed. Lawrenceville, GA: Committee for Christian Education and Publications, 1990.

Wimmer, A. C. "Bishops in Belgium Defy Vatican, Publish Ceremony for Blessing Same-Sex Unions." *Catholic News Agency*, September 20, 2022. https://www.catholicnewsagency.com/news/252339/belgium-bishops-defy-vatican-publish-ceremony-for-blessing-same-sex-unions.

www.ingramcontent.com/pod-product-compliance
Lightning Source LLC
Chambersburg PA
CBHW072146160426
43197CB00012B/2270